AMERICAN HIGHER EDUCATION

AMERICAN HIGHER EDUCATION

Servant of the People or Protector of Special Interests?

E. C. Wallenfeldt

Contributions to the Study of Education, Number 9

Greenwood Press
Westport, Connecticut • London, England

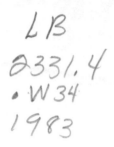

Library of Congress Cataloging in Publication Data

Wallenfeldt, E. C.
  American higher education.

  (Contributions to the study of education, ISSN 0196-
707X ; no. 9)
  Bibliography: p.
  Includes index.
  1. University autonomy—United States. 2. Higher
education and state—United States. 3. Universities
and colleges—United States—Administration. I. Title.
II. Series.
LB2331.4.W34 1983   378.73   82-15837
ISBN 0-313-23469-8 (lib. bdg.)

Library of Congress Catalog Card Number: 82-15837
ISBN: 0-313-23469-8
ISSN: 0196-707X

First published in 1983

Greenwood Press
A division of Congressional Information Service, Inc.
88 Post Road West
Westport, Connecticut 06881

Printed in the United States of America

10 9 8 7 6 5 4 3 2 1

SSH

CONTENTS

ACKNOWLEDGMENTS

Appreciation is expressed to colleagues Richard Bonnell, Dale Cook, Frank Cookingham, Pat Crisci, C. Brent DeVore, Charles Foreman, William Greenfield, William Konnert, Michael Malmisur, John Scigliano, J. Keith Varney, and Robert I. White for their provision of information and comments on various phases of this undertaking.

Special appreciation goes to colleague Fredrick Chambers for his critical reading of the manuscript and for the suggestions, information, ideas, and continuous support and encouragement he has provided.

INTRODUCTION

Recent publications about American colleges and universities have included comments, research reports, opinions, and theories on such topics as collective bargaining, affecting economies in institutional operations, schemes for financial support, interinstitutional cooperation and competition, affirmative action, managing a declining enterprise, strategic planning and evaluation, and the need for marketing higher education.

New vocabularies have evolved in many of these areas as specialized approaches are developed. The new language and increased specialization highlight the relevance of many of the assumptions and contentions associated with special interest group theories. Many groups have a legitimate claim on higher education, and colleges and universities, particularly those supported or assisted through public funds, traditionally have expressed the intent to serve the needs of a broad range of groups, constituencies, and "publics." However, many of the current writings concerning the condition of higher education today and the process by which it arrived there are not appropriate for a broad general audience. The language and content of these writings on higher education represent special interest perspectives, many of which tend to ignore, or regard as insignificant, basic realities and conditions influencing colleges and universities. The special interests responsible for many of the recent publications on higher education are themselves part of these realities and conditions. These special interests have tended to interpret from their own particular perspectives what is in the "public interest" or what is best for "the people."

If higher education is to reflect the needs of a broad range of groups and individuals, more communication is needed that attempts to transcend special interests and explains these interests and other realities and conditions that may not always surface in discussion of colleges and universities. This book is an effort to contribute to that communication. In this effort an attempt has been made to avoid the jargon that has come into use in a number of areas of higher education—it tends to confuse rather than clarify issues and approaches that should be understood by a wider group of people. The major emphasis is intended to be on realities and conditions of current times. However, where believed necessary to gain a better understanding of present situations, historical information is presented as background.

Chapter 1 presents a discussion of the nature of special interests or factions in American society and the system-wide influences of corporate power, militarization, racism, sexism, and over-quantification as they pertain to higher education. The external governance of colleges and universities is considered in Chapter 2, and the internal governance of these institutions is the topic of Chapter 3.

The funding of higher education, including state, federal, and private roles is examined in Chapter 4, business and financial operations are discussed in Chapter 5, and communication and public information, intercollegiate athletics, fund raising, and alumni relations are included under the heading "institutional advancement" in Chapter 6.

Accreditation and interinstitutional cooperation are the subjects of Chapter 7, the public service function is considered in Chapter 8, and planning and evaluation are discussed in Chapter 9.

It is hoped that this book provides some basic understandings for that broad audience of persons ignored by much of the literature in American higher education today.

AMERICAN HIGHER EDUCATION

1

SPECIAL INFLUENCES

All institutions in the United States, whether they relate to business, government, the administration of justice, welfare and social services, or education, have been affected by special interests and influences: corporate power, militarization, racism, sexism, and overquantification. (The latter condition is the idea that anything of value must have the capability of being measured and quantified.) It is appropriate to begin a discussion of American higher education with a consideration of this reality.

The Public and Special Interest

With deep roots in the *demos* of the ancient Greeks, the concept of public interest or general welfare is of long standing in American history. The phrase "to promote the general welfare" appears in the Preamble to the Constitution, the expression "commonwealth" is used officially in connection with governments of Kentucky, Massachusetts, Pennsylvania, and Virginia, and the word "commons" has come down through history as the place in the community where "the public" assembled to discuss its problems.

The concept of a "public" is apparent throughout the history of higher education in America. In colonial times and later, arguments for increased government involvement in the affairs of private institutions (Yale and Dartmouth) were based on making those colleges more receptive to the public.[1] A constitutional convention held in Michigan in June 1850 committed time and

energy to the consideration of the selection of persons serving
on the state university governing board, because it was believed
that the general public was not satisfied with the manner in
which the University of Michigan Regents were chosen and the
way they were operating the University.[2] Rationale advanced
by those favoring popularly elected trustees in that state, as
well as in Colorado, Illinois, Nebraska, and Nevada, related to
serving the public interest.

At the time the concept of public interest or general welfare
was recognized in the Constitution, there was a clear awareness
of "factions," what are now known as special interest groups.
The system of checks and balances in that document was an
effort to control "the mischiefs of faction."[3] Implied was a
realization that within the public are a number of diverse and
frequently conflicting views, each faction interpreting the common good from its own particular perspective.[4]

Such established statements as "all men are created equal"
and "with liberty and justice for all" are subject to different
interpretations. There is no common commitment to a standard
set of values that are held by all people. The struggle and tension
among factions, especially minorities and majorities, efforts
to compromise and adjust, and application of checks and balances are relied upon to balance rights, bring about change,
and maintain freedom. An accepted system of values implemented and enforced by a consensus government does not exist,
as might be expected from the language of the Preamble to the
Constitution. Individual rights and interests are not guaranteed,
but the opportunity to attain them is there in the system, at
least as an ideal. Attainment of rights and realization of interests
may involve, and even require, pragmatic methods and actions
that seem to violate the ideal for which the system purports
to stand.[5]

The system promotes behavior in which major social values
by individuals are accomplished through association with groups,
and there is a solid base of theory and research to support this
belief. These groups can be as basic as a juvenile gang or as complex as a multinational corporation, but the concept, nevertheless, as an influential force has become dominant in all social
sciences.[6] When groups become organized, they are structures

of power because they combine thinking ability, resourcefulness, strength, and action in an effort to accomplish their goals. Groups attempt to overcome obstacles in their environments when these barriers stand in the way of the attainment of their objectives. One of these obstacles actually may be the state or the government, itself a group that has gained official status because it represents a form of consensus. In the struggle that takes place among groups, those with greater organization tend to dominate. Effective organization requires knowledge and human and material resources, commodities more readily accessible to groups with financial means. This reality, combined with the tendency of groups to expand and become constantly more complex,[7] has resulted in the emergence of national corporations in the United States and powerful multinational corporations whose special interests prevail in international markets and economies. The power of these supercorporations appears to be operating without any effective checks and balances from international governments.[8]

Corporate Power

This development represents the international dimension of the concept of *corporate power*, a major system-wide influence on the political, social, and economic life of the United States. Control of the corporation is in the hands of a top-level management group, although many shareholders may have provided capital.[9] The power potential of this group that *is* the corporation is awesome, since the life of this country is dominated by business.[10] This domination in the realm of politics has been explored at the municipal community level through the research of Floyd Hunter. His conclusions and the extension of his thesis to the national level through further research are of particular significance for higher education. They show how moneyed special interests have a major impact on American institutions, including colleges and universities. Hunter studied political, social, and economic influences in Atlanta and concluded that major decisions concerning the politics, economics, and just about everything else that happened in that Georgia city were determined by people who represented the wealth and businesses

of that community. The lower-level bureaucracy, executing
rather than formulating policy, was made up in part of public
officials who were clearly in roles subordinate to the business
power elite.[11]

Hunter's concentration upon position, potential, and reputation was challenged by Robert A. Dahl on the basis of research at New Haven, Connecticut, where he studied the issues
of political nomination, public education, and urban renewal.
He found that different groups were influential in different
situations and called this phenomenon *pluralistic democracy*.[12]
He determined that it was interest, activity, and commitment
of time and energy which resulted in power and leadership.
This influence and leadership could change as issues changed.

The findings of Hunter and Dahl, probably the two major
theorists in community power, have been evaluated on the basis
of their research methods; Hunter's approach has been termed
"reputational" while Dahl's is called "decisional." It has been
contended that the power structure that emerges from the
study of a community will depend upon methods used to
investigate that structure. However, whether a reputational
analysis approach or an issue-oriented perspective is used, there
is evidence that both will find the same power system when
used in the same community.[13] The upper hand of the power
elites in Hunter's thesis has been supported when the importance
of issues is examined. Those issues that pluralistic leaders and
groups decide are probably those in which elites have little or
no interest. Elites do not become involved in those issues that
do not threaten their positions.[14]

Others have argued that communities, not methods, make
a difference. Therefore, pluralistic and elitist communities exist.
The pluralistic community is one in which many interest groups
function and there is little consensus concerning the general
direction in which the community should move. There is no
dominant value structure. The formal governing unit, represented by executive, legislative, and judicial branches, therefore,
appears to be a major source for the determination and resolution
of conflicts among groups. These groups can be seen working
at various points in the governing system with the result that
political power is spread and there is a diversification and spe-

cialization of organizational structures and services. On the other hand, the elitist type of community described by Hunter is characterized by consensus, shared values, and common views. The governmental structure is not as complex as that of the pluralistic community. Decision making is in the control of power elites and not too related to governmental structures.[15]

The direction of policies and programs of colleges and universities may be influenced by different forces depending upon the types of communities that affect them. However, as with any institution in American society, they will be influenced most by the groups that control finances. Granted that local differences exist in cities, and it is suspected that this applies to states and regions of the United States, economic influence is always a strong determinant whether that influence is based upon the wealth of home-owned businesses and industry or absentee corporate power. If economic power interests do not want an issue to come before the public, chances for that issue to reach the ballot box or even the newspaper headlines are slight. Politicians need money to campaign for public office and to retain that office once elected. The economic power elite positions and potential become realities when the interests of the elites are threatened, whether or not that elite is a specifically identifiable group or an abstract concept.

For colleges and universities, this economic power elite has special significance at the corporate level. Hunter, in the projection of his thesis to the national level, found that business corporations are vital forces in every aspect of American life, controlling politics at local, state, and national levels in all areas that affect the business community and its special interests; these interests frequently run counter to the interests of other groups, maybe even the majority of all other groups.[16]

In higher education, the important position of corporate power in all its dimensions—manufacturing, marketing, investing, and other areas—has long been apparent. Industrialists and financiers with names like Rockefeller, Carnegie, Vanderbilt, Mellon, and Stanford built universities. In the 1920s, boards of trustees were dominated by corporate leaders. For example the Board of Trustees of Columbia University, in addition to the institution's president, a bishop, a physician, and an engineer,

included ten corporation lawyers and other persons categorized
as bankers, railroad owners, real estate owners, merchants, and
manufacturers, all of whom had some connection with J. P.
Morgan.[17] The banking firm of Lee, Higginson, and Company
was influential on the board at Harvard,[18] and the University
of Pennsylvania board included a number of persons with connections in the United Gas Improvement Company.[19]

In the 1930s, a study of 734 board members from 30 leading
colleges and universities revealed that 46 percent of these members served on boards of directors of businesses; 15.4 percent
were bankers, brokers, and financiers; 15.5 percent were classified as "manufacturing entrepreneurs and executives"; 5.9 percent
were "dealers and transportation officials"; 1.6 percent were
involved in the insurance business; 1.1 percent dealt in real
estate; and 2.0 percent were participants in other businesses.
The latter included the president of Standard Oil of New Jersey
and another oil company president, an executive of Shell Oil,
the chief executive of a large copper company and another
mining company president, the president of the Consolidated
Coal Company, and four presidents of construction companies.[20]

Corporate leaders continue to be in positions of influence
in higher education. In 1977 the results of a survey by the
American Council on Education and the Association of Governing Boards showed that 34.5 percent of board members
were active business and industrial executives. Over 50 percent
of those executives were presidents of corporations or served
as heads of the boards of directors of corporations. The next
highest occupational category (10.1 percent) consisted of clergy,
but the third and fourth highest categories were lawyers (8.4
percent) and physicians and dentists (5.5 percent) respectively.
Undoubtedly a substantial number of physicians and dentists
have incorporated their practices, and some attorneys serve
corporations.[21]

The involvement of the corporate sector in colleges and
universities has had another significant influence that relates
to the spirit of discovery and inquiry, hallmarks of the ideology
of American higher education, and also to its financial support.
The practice through which major research universities either
invest in or actually establish private biotechnology companies,

which are in business for profit, has received considerable attention in recent years. Both universities as institutions and professors as individuals can increase their income through the profits companies realize as a result of university research. For example, biomedical research might produce a medicine that cures a particular illness. While the public in general benefits from this cure, the pharmaceutical or chemical company that has sponsored the research producing it and holds the patent stands to profit financially. The professor or institution who has an investment in the company also receives a financial reward. In some instances the research that produces the profit-making product has been partially supported through federal or state funds granted to the researcher or the researching institution. This situation can produce a conflict between public and private interests. Relevant to this problem, Jonathan King, Professor of Biology at the Massachusetts Institute of Technology, pointed out at the annual convention of the American Association for the Advancement of Science in 1982 that public support should be denied to such ventures. When companies charge the public for the products of research, people are paying twice, since their tax dollars helped to support the research.

More significantly, King argued that a researcher who stands to profit financially from his findings may not share the results of these findings with his colleagues for fear that they might then make discoveries that would capture a share of the market. The open sharing that has helped the advancement of knowledge will be impaired, the spirit of scientific inquiry will be stifled, the special interests of individuals will conflict with the public interest, and the obligations of universities to advance knowledge and improve the human condition will be compromised.[22]

It is difficult to deny that there is a strong corporate and business influence on the policies, programs, and practices of colleges and universities. Any attempts to understand American higher education must recognize that the special interests of business and the corporate sector are probably the most significant determinants on the directions that college and university developments take, just as they are on all other institutions in American society. As Calvin Coolidge said so many years ago, "the business of America is business."[23]

Militarization

Another system-wide influence somewhat akin to corporate power is that of *militarization*. Armed conflict, the threat of war, and the building of defenses to avert actual hostilities have been vital factors in the shaping of the life and destiny of America, and this has very much included higher education. The country was established through a violent revolution, maintained through strife with the British in 1812, expanded through the Mexican War, matured, preserved, and held accountable for its commitments by the Civil War, expanded again through the Spanish-American War, placed in the international arena through World War I, elevated from the depths of economic and social-psychological depression and reaffirmed as an important force in world affairs by the Second World War, had its dignity maintained through a showing of restraint in the Korean War, and divided in spirit and philosophy and humbled through defeat in battle as well as ideology in Vietnam.

Since the advent of the cold war with the Eastern bloc nations in 1949, the maintenance of a strong defense as deterence against aggression has been the foremost concern of those responsible for the national budget. Prior to the beginning of the cold war, another development took place which has established a pattern for the involvement of the military in a major way in the corporate world as well as in government. Immediately following World War II, a nation that was shifting from a wartime to a peacetime economy needed leadership to direct the transition. Individuals who had capability for strategic planning and logistics related to the redirection of massive human and material resources were required in top-level administrative positions in industry and in government. Military leaders appeared to have the necessary qualifications for this task. Although selected first by an educational institution, Columbia University, to redirect its efforts in this new era, the man who led the "Great Crusade" in Europe emerged as the governmental chief executive. His election as President of the United States represented a trend that continues to have import, although this influence has peaked and ebbed from time to time. The election of Dwight D. Eisenhower as the thirty-fourth

President of the United States perhaps was the major event in
a pattern that has seen military leaders move to executive positions in government and industry. This system of interaction
has seen former generals negotiate and lobby for top defense
contracts as representatives of principal corporations. Knowledge
of the military and established friendships have been significant
in these negotiations. A close relationship has been maintained
between the military establishment and the corporate powers.
Eisenhower warned of the dangers of this military-industrial
complex when he left office over twenty years ago, but its
influence remains.[24]

The massive defense industry created by the military-industrial complex has had particular implications for higher education because it draws from the efforts of some of the best
minds in the country. Experts in the colleges and universities
direct their energies to defense-related research and development
rather than an application of science and technology to the
broader problems of humankind related to survival in the future
as the environment becomes polluted and energy sources are
exhausted.[25] The activities of researchers and scholars require
financial support and, if the major share of that money comes as
a result of the arms economy, the principal share of research will
be in the direction of defense.

Further examination of the influence of militarization reveals
that the funding of higher education by the federal government
has come about essentially because of war, threat of war, or
some type of defense needs. The subject of federal government
involvement in higher education is discussed at a later point, but
it is appropriate in the consideration of militarization to say
that one of the stipulations for the awarding of extensive land-
grant funds for colleges of agriculture and mechanic arts in
1862 was that programs for the training of military officers
also be provided. While perhaps not a major consideration, the
effects of the Civil War were, nonetheless, apparent. During
World War I, students in medicine, science, and technology
were excused from military service because these areas were
thought vital to the American war effort. Military training
programs were also expanded on college and university campuses
and were responsible for the first type of federal financial as-

sistance that went to private institutions. Military training programs reached massive proportions during the Second World War. It has been estimated that many men's colleges received as much as 50 percent of the support of their operating expenses from contracts with the Army and Navy in 1945.[26]

Government defense research needs were met through programs in its own laboratories for the most part until World War II.[27] However, defense research was conducted using university resources and facilities during World War I. For example, James B. Conant, who became well-known as a member of the research team developing the atomic bomb in the 1940s, as the President of Harvard, and as United States Ambassador to the Federal Republic of Germany, was a member of a group of organic chemists conducting chemical warfare research at the American University in 1917-1918.[28] In the early 1940s, research on weapons and weapons systems by institutions of higher learning was extensive. It was conducted under the general direction of the National Defense Research Commission, an agency established by President Franklin Roosevelt to mobilize and coordinate the activities of the scientific community in the war effort. Two leaders from higher education served on the Commission— Conant, as a chemist and President of Harvard, and Karl T. Compton, a physicist and President of the Massachusetts Institute of Technology. Other scientists on the Commission were its chair Vannevar Bush, President of the Carnegie Institution of Washington; Frank B. Jewett, President of the National Academy of Science; and Richard Tolman, a professor of physics from the California Institute of Technology.[29]

Higher education has continued to be involved in aspects of defense research, but this participation has been more subject to controversy during peacetime years. Although the close relationship between some colleges and universities and the Department of Defense has been questioned,[30] funds going to institutions of higher education for research related to national defense have increased. The administration's proposed budget for fiscal year 1983 for the National Science Foundation represented a 7.4 percent increase over the 1982 year with the major part of the increase in this $1.077 billion budget going

to the areas of computer science and robotics. These areas have
crucial significance for national defense.[31]

World War II was responsible for the first extensive federal
aid program for students. Through the Servicemen's Readjust-
ment Act, better known as the G.I. Bill, thousands of veterans
received money to attend college. A similar bill provided assistance
for Korean War veterans to participate in higher education in
the 1950s and 1960s.

The indirect threat of military aggression from the Soviet
Union prompted the National Defense Education Act of 1958.
The Soviet launching of the *Sputnik* spaceship in 1957 caused
Americans to believe that the United States had dropped behind
the Soviet Union in the production of scientific brainpower.
The Act provided funds for the education of persons studying
science, foreign languages, mathematics, and other disciplines
believed essential to the national defense.[32] Thousands of persons have been educated through provisions of this act.

Racism

The education at all levels of thousands of persons in the
United States has also been affected by another system-wide
condition influencing all American institutions. That condition,
racism, has its foundations in the economic institution of slavery.
The economy of slavery established the idea that blacks were
inferior to whites and not capable of participating in the main-
stream of activities of American society. There were signers of
the Declaration of Independence such as John Adams and
Thomas Jefferson who saw inconsistencies between the spirit
and language of that document and the institution of slavery.
However, they feared that Southern leaders would not approve
the elimination of slavery and hence not support the new nation.[33]
Economic interests won out over human interests and may have
set a precedent that prevails today in American society.

While slavery was terminated with the Emancipation Procla-
mation, prejudice against blacks has continued. Racial prejudice
and discrimination have been recognized as unfair and unjust
for many years, but it is just within the past two decades that

the institutionalized and system-wide nature of this problem has received attention. Because of the broad application of this situation, blacks have been denied opportunities to participate in policy and decision making at all levels of government. Talented and resourceful persons have had to overcome severe odds to realize their potentials because of discrimination in business, labor organizations, welfare and justice programs, and in education.[34] Subtle and sometimes not so subtle discriminatory practices have been apparent even though a preponderance of scientific evidence clearly refutes all claims of black inferiority.

In the area of higher education, it was not until 1850 that a black studied at Harvard, the most prestigious of all American colleges; Martin R. Delany attended medical school there in 1850-1851. The first black graduate of that institution, Richard Greener, completed his degree in 1870. W.E.B. Du Bois, an early advocate of political and social justice for blacks, was probably the most famous black graduate of a major university in the nineteenth century. He graduated in 1890 and has written of the social segregation and isolation he experienced at the Harvard fountainhead of enlightenment.[35]

In the years after the Civil War, black attendance at colleges and universities in the North increased, but most blacks were being educated at institutions in the South. John Sekora provides a revealing summary of the situation of these institutions and also for blacks in general:

> For a hundred years the students and teachers at Negro colleges have indeed been anomalous within the system of American higher education. They have not shared in the protection, security, prosperity, or camaraderie available to their white colleagues. The anamoly has in fact been so great that it is historically false to speak of Negro colleges as *within* the academic community. Rather they have been as pariahs to the community or as the unacknowledged bastard children of a righteous household. Today, as in 1880, Southern Negro colleges stand in the same derivative condition as the Northern urban

ghettoes. White institutions created them, white
institutions controlled them, white institutions
maintained them, and white institutions degraded
them.[36]

Evidence of racism in higher education is apparent in discussion of the status of blacks in professions. In considering
the number of persons in professional fields requiring advanced
degrees, there is not a single field in which more than 3 percent
of the members are black. Such closed societies as the American
Medical Association and the American Bar Association have
sole authority for licensing individuals to practice medicine and
law respectively. Further, National Science Foundation Manpower Characteristics System statistics of 1973 indicate that
of 226,750 persons holding doctoral degrees and employed as
physical scientists, mathematical scientists, computer specialists,
environmental scientists, engineers, life scientists, psychologists,
and social scientists only 1,700 were black.[37]

In the late 1960s and early 1970s black student, faculty,
and staff protests against discriminatory practices in higher
education were widespread. Action was taken in a number of
institutions to compensate for past errors in ignoring the contribution of blacks to American society. Greater emphasis on
black culture came about and efforts were made to provide
more opportunities for blacks and other minorities to participate
in higher education as students, faculty, staff, and administrators.
However, in spite of some progress there is evidence that problems persist. In East Lansing, Michigan, in 1982, 350 black
faculty, students, and alumni were present at the January
meeting of the Michigan State University Board of Trustees to
show their concern over institutional conditions related to
blacks:

Nearly a dozen speakers at the January meeting
expressed frustration over the small number of
minority faculty and staff, a decline in the number
of black students, increased incidents of racial
hostility and the absence of black faculty in the
Department of Theatre and James Madison College.[38]

The annual affirmative action report indicated that, for minorities represented among academic and nonacademic employees, percentages and numbers had increased even though the number of positions actually available had gone down. A decrease from 3.5 to 3.4 percent was reported for the percentage of blacks in academic ranks "with an increase in proportional representation for tenure system faculty and continuing staff and a decrease in the representation of temporary faculty and staff." Forty-five percent of the new persons entering the tenure track system were from minorities or were nonminority women. Defined as faculty problem areas for 1981-1982 were retaining minorities and adding more blacks in the areas of agriculture, biological and physical sciences, and engineering.[39]

An indication of the persistence of racial problems might be illustrated through mention of policy for the financial support of two-year higher educational programs in Mississippi. Community college funding policies in that state have had a subtle influence on attendance practices. Six percent of state allocations go to colleges on the basis of a flat grant. Every college receives the same amount of dollars under this plan. However 94 percent of state funds are awarded on the basis of the number of full-time day students attending academic as opposed to vocational-technical programs. The indication is clear that the intention of this plan is not to use state tax dollars to support programs for part-time vocational-technical students in community colleges. As a result, community colleges have become university-parallel program centers and students with vocational-technical preparation interests have tended to enroll at area vocational education centers. Community colleges appear to be attended by mostly white students, and vocational education centers have been predominantly black institutions.[40]

An indicator that probably has the most significant implications in terms of the influence of blacks on American higher education is the number of blacks serving on boards of trustees, the top governing agencies in American higher education. In 1977 studies of board members at four-year institutions, community colleges, and predominantly black colleges and universities were reported. Of the 47,138 trustees and regents on the 2,314 boards governing 3,037 campuses, only 5 percent of

board membership for privately financed institutions were
black while blacks represented only 11 percent of trustees or
regents on publicly assisted single-campus boards. In the case
of predominantly black colleges, 62 percent of board members
were white. Those studies also showed that 15 percent of the
trustees on private single campus boards were women while
18 percent of the membership of single-campus public boards
were female.[41]

Sexism

If the condition of blacks in terms of influence upon higher
education is minimal, the impact of women on policies, programs,
and practices is perhaps even less. *Sexism* is a major point of
contention in American society in general, but especially significant for what is taking place in colleges and universities.

For decades American women have found themselves in a
situation of subservience to men. There has been a general
cultural expectation that their major roles be in childrearing,
family maintenance, and other domestic tasks. Their satisfaction
was to come from the accomplishments and happiness of their
husbands. They were not expected to enter career areas and
professions in which they would be in competition with men,
and when they did, they experienced severe discrimination
and prejudice. This situation was reinforced through the media,
business practices and policies, politics at all levels, and in
education. Women who wished to establish an identity that
differed from the cultural expectation faced constant opposition.
From time to time, various efforts toward equality of rights and
opportunities were made by individuals and groups who realized
the injustice of the situation and the loss and waste of valuable
human resources that it represented for society.[42]

A concerted effort has come about in the middle and late
1960s to develop equal rights and opportunities for women,
and this movement has continued into the 1970s and 1980s,
experiencing a series of gains and setbacks. In society in general,
women are still behind men in terms of such areas as salaries
and wages. In 1977 the median income for men who were
employed full-time on a year-round basis was $15,070, while

women in comparable status had a median income of only
$8,814.[43] Women, although they have been involved in political
campaigns and organizations, have had difficulty in gaining
elected office and positions of power and authority. A number
of myths about their personalities, interests, and abilities have
been responsible for this.[44]

In higher education, few women have attained chief executive officer positions. Approximately 2,365 two-year and four-year institutions of higher education were listed in 1982 in *The World
Almanac and Book of Facts.* Of the chief executives of these
colleges and universities, all enrolling 200 or more students,
fewer than 8 percent were women.[45] Women faculty members
appear not to have fared much better. The point has been made
that two general assumptions seem to be held in colleges and
universities concerning faculty performance. The first is that
women are not as serious about their professional lives as men,
and the second that they do not have the professional dedication
and actual ability men possess. This results in the conclusion
that women can not compete with men in the area of scholarly
publication and, therefore, should not advance in rank because
scholarly productivity is the major basis for promotion.[46]

It has also been said that men appear to control positions on
institutional and American Association of University Professors
committees, which hear women's grievances. Further, the claim
has been made that it is difficult for women to receive fair treatment if they seek justice through the courts. The system allows
the judge to impose an individual sense of justice, ignore evidence,
and avoid a strict interpretation of the letter of the law and
instead rule in a manner that maintains the position of the
woman as subordinate to men.[47] An additional contention has
been that the Higher Education Division of the Office of Civil
Rights has not been effective in enforcement because of the
extensive indifference it has encountered. Furthermore, little
success has been achieved by the Equal Employment Opportunity Commission.[48]

To support the position that women have been underrepre-
sented in the upper faculty ranks, a 1971 survey of modern
language departments of 418 colleges and universities can be

cited. That survey, conducted by the Modern Language Association Commission on the Status of Women in the Professions,
revealed that 49 percent of modern language instructors and
lecturers are women, but women constitute only 7 percent of
persons who have reached the rank of full professor. Other
evidence of apparent discrimination against women is seen in
the fact that appointments of women to positions in colleges
and universities increased by only nine-tenths of 1 percent, or
19.1 to 20.0 percent, from 1968 to 1972, even though affirmative action guidelines and court actions were supposed to have
accelerated this trend. Also, 19 percent of all male employees
in higher education received salaries of $17,000 or higher in
1968. During that same year only 4 percent of women employees were at that level or better. This discrepancy continues,[49]
and society will continue to be the loser until the strengths,
competencies, and interests of women as individuals are recognized free from preconceived and stereotyped ideas concerning
what women should and should not be.

Overquantification

Preconceived notions have had an influence of widespread
importance for higher education, if not American society in
general, in another respect. The idea is that all aspects of life
can be calculated, measured, and determined by weighing one
set of numbers against another with the ultimate answers being
obvious to everyone, since certain numbers are always higher
than others. The solution yielding the higher numerical value
emerges as the only answer. The attractiveness of this approach
is difficult to deny. It covers the best in scientific advancement
because it specifies that direct observation is necessary and
must be accompanied with a recording of observations, exactly
as noted by the observer. If the majority of persons observing
a particular event or development seem to agree, the conclusion
they reach has to be better than other answers that are obtained
through different methods. While direct observation and the
actual measurement of results represent a strategic advancement in modern science—a breakthrough from mysticism and

divine inspiration as ultimates—this approach needs to be kept in perspective without denying that exact measurement and evaluation should be constant goals. Decisions and judgments should be made on the basis of fact or irrefutable evidence. However, how that evidence is obtained and how conclusions are drawn should be subjected to careful examination before irretractable action is taken, and even if this action is taken, there should be a perspective that allows for its reconsideration.

The understanding of problems as well as potentials in this area requires recognition of the basis for knowledge, since a modern world and a modern system of education both express a commitment to reason based on facts. This understanding relates to more than a definition of knowledge; it concerns the process through which knowledge is formed and perceived. As hard as it may be for the objective scientist to accept, knowledge in its ultimate and most significant form is based upon individual experience, beliefs, and values.

The fundamental "belief" nature of knowledge can be explored through a review of some major approaches to epistemology. Some "leaps in faith" are important considerations when philosophical roots are considered. Some central philosophical positions can present a convincing argument for the affective (emotional-feeling) nature of knowledge. This argument focuses on, first, the process through which knowledge emerges as it relates directly to observable events, and, second, knowledge pertaining to the unobservable and the future. This review of central positions concerns a person's ability to know what is really happening around him or her, the nature of the mental process through which he or she comes to know what is happening, and whether what that person concludes is going on is really what is happening. A continuum or scale of belief might be used to address these concerns. Thomas Huxley's agnosticism occupies one end, and the more widely held affirmation that people do have some knowledge of reality claims the opposite end. While Huxley's position is that comprehension of reality is impossible, the skepticism of David Hume moves closer to a position that it might be possible for human beings to understand the nature of their world. Hume expressed doubt that humankind could know reality, but he left the door open for that possibility.[50]

Whether a skeptical, affirmative, or agnostic position is taken on humankind's ability to know reality, philosophers have expressed concern over the manner in which reality might be known. The way that people come to know reality, or in a more contemporary context, life, is important. Instruments of knowledge, or in other words, the way people attempt to answer questions about the meaning of life, might be placed in five categories: (1) sense-perceptual experience, (2) reason, (3) intuition, (4) authority, and (5) revelation.[51]

The elements of faith and belief are readily apparent in intuition, authority, and revelation, but reason and sense-perceptual experience require closer examination to support the contention that their roots are affective. Sense-perceptual experience and reason appear to be the principal instruments of knowledge in education. The establishment of the faith-belief basis for these instruments requires consideration of positions supported by John Locke and David Hume.

Locke's empiricist position related sensory testing to reason. He believed knowledge is derived from the experience of direct perception. Ideas and concepts are formed in the mind from experience and the actual examination of observation in nature. Since true knowledge has to be verified through observations, Locke inserted the concept of judgment to provide linkages between observable events when direct observation itself could not furnish those connections. Locke defined judgment as the "faculty which God has given man to supply the want of clear and certain knowledge" and he insisted "that man would be at a great loss if he had nothing to direct him but what was the certainty of true knowledge."[52] Locke's concept of judgment, though ambiguous, is more in the realm of faith and belief than in the domain of certainty.

Hume has added a caution, which needs to be considered in the making of judgments. He asserted that "There is no process of reasoning which provides that the qualities of objects and the effects of their use will always be the same as the first experience with them."[53] He submits further that "If we be, therefore, engaged by arguments to put trust in past experience, and make it the standard for our future judgement, these arguments must be probable only."[54] Hume recognized that judgment is based on probability and that belief and faith are important components of the probable. Hume's position requires a belief, and it provides an excellent base for connecting knowledge to belief through recognition of the process of perception. Concerning Hume's view of perception, it has been stated:

> Hume's psychological theories of concept formation
> and induction establish the conditions that must be
> satisfied in order for us to make factually significant
> statements and generally reliable inductive references.
> The possibility of knowledge is limited by these
> conditions, which is why epistemology is not inde-
> pendent of psychology.[55]

Hume maintained that knowledge comes from impressions—marks or effects etched in the human mind through perceptions of actual experience—and from ideas which are copies of these impressions. Simple ideas are formed on basic sensations, and complex ideas come from a mixture of complex impressions or simple ideas.[56] The activity through which ideas are formulated involves not only the senses, but habit, instinct, and feeling.[57] "In short, all materials of thinking are derived from outward or inward sentiment; the mixture and composition of these belongs alone to the mind and will."[58] There are no ideas without impressions. Because these ideas are illusionary and based upon impressions rather than absolutes, they are subjective and tentative in nature and dependent upon individual perception, feeling, and experience. Therefore, when inferences about the future are made, they are "leaps in faith" because of conditions in nature in the external world, as well as because of the manner in which ideas are formed.

If what Hume has said makes sense, knowledge is belief and is, at the highest point in the human mind, subjective and affective rather than in the cognitive domain. Knowledge changes as impressions, observations, ideas, conditions, and people change. It is flexible, not rigid and fixed.

Educational leaders have a tendency, perhaps more unconsciously than consciously, to regard knowledge as an absolute; their theories while initially tentative become crystalized and all-encompassing, and they consider most characteristics of reality as measurable. They give properties to events and activities and imply an exactness and simplicity of solution that does not exist. The belief-faith foundation of knowledge should not be overlooked. The "grain of salt" which Hume has provided concerning the nature of knowledge must be kept in mind, if a proper perspective is to be maintained and higher education, past, present, and future, is to be understood.

Summary

The influences of corporate power, militarization, racism, sexism, and overquantification are important factors to consider in any effort to understand American higher education. Above all they affect special interests as these interests have shaped higher education in the past, are influencing it in the present, and will affect its future.

Notes

1. John S. Brubacher and Willis Rudy, *Higher Education in Transition: A History of American Colleges and Universities, 1636-1976*, 3d. ed. rev. and enl. (New York: Harper and Row, 1976), pp. 32-34.

2. Howard W. Peckham, *The Making of the University of Michigan, 1817-1967* (Ann Arbor, Michigan: University of Michigan Press, 1967), p. 32.

3. Betty H. Zisk, *Local Interest Politics: A One-Way Street* (Indianapolis, Indiana: Bobbs-Merrill, 1973), p. 1.

4. William F. Ogburn and Meyer F. Nimkoff, *Sociology* (Boston: Houghton Mifflin, 1940), pp. 282-283.

5. Lewis M. Killian, *The Impossible Revolution* (New York: Random House, 1968), pp. 10-13.

6. Earl Latham, "The Group Basis of Politics," in *American Political Interest Groups: Readings in Theory and Research*, ed. Betty H. Zisk (Belmont, California: Wadsworth, 1969), pp. 17-19.

7. Ibid., pp. 23-28.

8. Sumner Rosen, ed., *Economic Power Failure* (New York: McGraw-Hill, 1974), pp. 165-166.

9. Jerome H. Skolnik and Elliott Currie, eds., *Crisis in American Institutions* (Boston: Little, Brown, 1970), p. 122.

10. Rosen, *Economic Power Failure*, pp. 15-16.

11. Floyd Hunter, *Community Power Structure* (Chapel Hill, North Carolina: University of North Carolina Press, 1953), p. 113.

12. Robert A. Dahl, *Who Governs?* (New Haven, Connecticut: Yale University Press, 1961), pp. 89-91.

13. Robert E. Agger and Daniel Goldrich, "Community Power Structures and Partisanship," *American Sociological Review* 23 (August 1958): 383-392.

14. Frank W. Lutz, "Methods and Conceptualizations of Power in Education," in *The Politics of Education*, ed. Jay D. Scribner (Chicago: National Society for the Study of Education, 1977), p. 37.

15. Laurence Iannaconne, *Educational Policy Systems: A Study Guide for Educational Administrators* (Fort Lauderdale, Florida: Nova University Press, 1975), pp. 89-92.

16. Floyd Hunter, *Top Leadership, U.S.A.* (Chapel Hill, North Carolina: University of North Carolina Press, 1959), pp. 252-254.

17. Upton Sinclair, *The Goose Step: A Study of American Education* (Pasadena, California: Upton Sinclair, 1923), p. 25.

18. Ibid., p. 62.

19. Ibid., p. 93.

20. Hubert P. Beck, *Men Who Control Our Universities* (Morningside Heights, New York: King's Crown Press, 1947), pp. 48-52.

21. Jack Magarrell, "Who Controls the Universities?" *Chronicle of Higher Education*, September 6, 1977, p. 7.

22. Kim McDonald, "Commercialization of University Science is Decried," *Chronicle of Higher Education*, January 13, 1982, p. 9.

23. Merle Curti, *The Growth of American Thought*, 2d. ed. (New York: Harper and Brothers, 1951), p. 693.

24. David M. Shoup, "The New American Militarism," in *Crisis in American Institutions*, ed. Jerome H. Skolnik and Elliott Currie (Boston: Little, Brown, 1970), p. 170.

25. Rosen, *Economic Power Failure*, p. 9.

26. Brubacher and Rudy, *Higher Education in Transition*, pp. 224-225.

27. American Assembly, Columbia University, *The Federal Government and Higher Education* (Englewood Cliffs, New Jersey: Prentice-Hall, 1960), p. 78.

28. James B. Conant, *My Several Lives* (New York: Harper and Row, 1970), pp. 48-49.

29. Ibid., pp. 234-247.

30. Ibid., pp. 244.

31. "Scientific Research," *Chronicle of Higher Education*, February 17, 1982, p. 18.

32. American Assembly, Columbia University, *The Federal Government and Higher Education*, pp. 33-34.

33. Killian, *The Impossible Revolution*, p. 26.

34. Skolnik and Currie, *Crisis in American Institutions*, pp. 70-74.

35. Marcia G. Synnot, *The Half-Opened Door* (Westport, Connecticut: Greenwood Press, 1979), p. 48.

36. John Sekora, "Murder Relentless and Impassive: The American Academic Community and the Negro College," *Soundings* 51 (Fall 1968): 252.

37. Lorenzo Morris, *Elusive Equality: The Status of Black Americans in Higher Education* (Washington, D. C.: Howard University Press, 1979), pp. 206-207.

38."Blacks Respond to Affirmative Action Report," *MSU Today: For Alumni and Friends of Michigan State University* 1, no. 3 (February 1982): 2.

39. Ibid.

40. Walter L. Garms, *Financing Community Colleges* (New York: Teachers College Press, 1977), p. 106.

41. Magarrell, "Who Controls the Universities?" p. 7.

42. Betty Friedan, *The Feminine Mystique* (New York: Dell Publishing, 1963), pp. 1-27.

43. Margaret A. Berger, *Litigation on Behalf of Women: A Review for the Ford Foundation* (New York: Ford Foundation, 1980), p. 10.

44. Cynthia F. Epstein, "Women and Power: The Roles of Women in Politics in the United States," in *Access to Power: Cross-National Studies of Women and Elites*, ed. Cynthia F. Epstein and Rose L. Coser (London: George Allen and Unwin, 1981), pp. 124-126.

45. Newspaper Enterprise Association, *The World Almanac and Book of Facts 1982* (New York: Newspaper Enterprise Association, 1982), pp. 165-188.

46. Joan Abramson, *The Invisible Woman* (San Francisco: Jossey-Bass, 1975), p. 69.

47. Ibid., pp. 215-216.

48. Ibid., p. 185.

49. Betty Richardson, *Sexism in Higher Education* (New York: Continuum Book-Seabury Press, 1974), pp. 16-17.

50. Steven C. Jessie, "The Nature of Knowledge and Its Implications for Mental Health" (Ph.D. diss., Kent State University, 1976), pp. 1-14.

51. J. Donald Butler, *Four Philosophies and Their Practice in Education and Religion* (New York: Harper and Brothers, 1957), p. 27.

52. John Locke, "An Essay Concerning Human Understanding," in *Great Books of the Western World*, vol. 35, ed. Robert M. Hutchins (Chicago: Encyclopedia Britannica, 1952), p. 364.

53. Jessie, "The Nature of Knowledge and Its Implications for Mental Health," p. 26.

54. David Hume, "An Enquiry Concerning Human Understanding," in *Great Books of the Western World*, vol. 35, ed. Robert M. Hutchins (Chicago: Encyclopedia Britannica, 1952), p. 462.

55. James Noxon, "Hume's Concern With Religion," in *David Hume, Many-Sided Genius*, ed. Kenneth R. Merrill and Robert W. Shahan (Norman, Oklahoma: University of Oklahoma Press, 1976), pp. 63-64.

56. Jessie, "The Nature of Knowledge and Its Implications for Mental Health," pp. 27-30; Noxon, "Hume's Concern With Religion," pp. 63-64.

57. Noxon, "Hume's Concern With Religion," p. 67.

58. Hume, "An Enquiry Concerning Human Understanding," p. 456.

2

EXTERNAL GOVERNANCE

The forms and practices of external governance that exist today in higher education reflect the legacy of the private corporate model established through the Dartmouth Case. The external governance of colleges and universities has also been influenced by developments that are characteristic of all service organizations. Certain trends and problems have had an important bearing on the patterns of control that have emerged and the relationship between governing boards and state governmental authorities.

In general the responsibilities of board members have remained constant with the exception that long-range planning and research have become more important as bases for policy making as financial resources decrease. The membership of boards has become more representative of society in recent years, but business and industrial leaders and professional people are still dominant.

This chapter examines more recent characteristics, trends, responsibilities, and problems relating to the boards of trustees controlling American higher education.

The Dartmouth Legacy and Change

The manner in which institutions were first chartered provided a structure for external governance that was like that of a private business corporation. The United States Supreme Court in the case of the *Trustees of Dartmouth College* v. *Woodward* reaffirmed that status in a decision that established

that colleges were relatively immune from state or federal government intervention on behalf of public interests. Regardless
of whether institutions were under private or public control,
they were governed by corporations of persons who were not
in residence on the campuses and one administrator who was.
The universities in Scotland and in the Netherlands had external
boards of control in an official sense, but these groups did not
exert the influence typical of American boards. English universities and most of those on the continent of Europe, while
originating under church control, were influenced extensively
by faculty. The nonresident nature of American boards resulted
in their delegation of considerable authority to presidents who
managed day-to-day operations, made required decisions, and
emerged as powerful administrative officials having no exact
counterpart in the universities in Europe.

The corporate style of operation has been reinforced over the
years because board members have tended to come from the
ranks of the wealthy. These persons have been no strangers to
corporate management in the business sector. Even though
board members have functioned in a manner similar to directors
of a corporation responsible for the interests of shareholders,
other conditions evolving from traditions of higher education
and economic developments have tended to mitigate board
authority. The power of the institutional president emerging
in the American system and the strategic position of this person
in influencing board member opinion and action have served as
a restraint on board power. Since the board has the authority
to appoint and remove the president, it, in turn, has balanced
the power of the person in that position. Although presidents
and boards are major sources of power, the English tradition
of strong faculty involvement has not died in the United States.
Faculty councils and senates have come into existence and
exercise varying degrees of influence, principally in the areas of
standards for admission of students, curriculum and instruction,
academic standards and degree requirements, and research.
Faculty collective bargaining groups have arisen with major
effects in the areas of appointment, promotion, salary increases,
and other academic personnel matters. Alumni have exerted
various degrees of influence, both as individuals and through

organized groups. Nonacademic personnel (classified service staff members) have gained increased representation on advisory committees and task forces. During the later 1960s and early 1970s, the student voice was strong, and disruptive activities on college campuses had impacts on boards and presidents. Other groups more external to the institutions have also been factors.[1]

The tradition of academic freedom, which developed in American colleges and universities through the land-grant act and German influences on graduate education and research, necessitated boards acting in the role of buffer between the institution and special interest groups in society, including state and federal government elements. A most difficult task for boards has become preserving higher education's ability to analyze society's problems critically in the face of strong opposition from special interest groups.[2] In times of limited tax dollars for public higher education, legislators who are responsible to the voters for wise expenditures of these funds have demanded increased involvement in the affairs of colleges and universities. They have challenged the authority of boards. Since the time of the Dartmouth Case, court action has caused colleges and universities to become more accountable to the public. Increased interest in constitutional rights and protections has resulted in greater court involvement in the affairs of educational institutions.

Vestiges of the private corporate model remain, but changing conditions in society have made a difference in the external governance of American higher education.

Institutions of Higher Education as Service Organizations

An external system of governance, given these circumstances, encounters problems in a complex society, but the need for such control must be emphasized and maintained in spite of these problems. A somewhat oversimplified pronouncement on the situation points out that without external control, survival needs in service organizations like colleges and universities become more important than the ends those organizations are supposed to serve.

To understand this, it must be accepted that all organizations of, by, and for human beings are either service organizations whose purpose is to serve the needs of individuals and groups outside that organization, or they are self-serving organizations, which have the goal of promoting the interests of their own members. The first category of organization includes hospitals, city councils, state legislatures, the Congress of the United States, the Air Force, Army, Navy, and colleges and universities. Families, neighborhood gangs, community action councils at one end of a continuum and country clubs and the American Medical Association at the other are examples of self-serving organizations, although members of the latter may disagree with this classification for their group.

Problems arise for persons whose needs are to be met by service organizations because there is a fundamental tendency in the human character, singly and collectively, to promote self-interest. This means that the first classification of groups, the service organization, becomes like the second type of organization. The service organization, if not checked through some action or structure in the system, will direct its efforts to the survival needs and self-interests of its immediate members. The original purpose, to serve those outside the organization, will tend to be sacrificed.[3]

There are two principal implications arising from this situation. The first concerns board membership, and the second relates to the responsibility of boards to see that their institutions do not become self-serving, narcissistic ivory towers that are isolated from the realities and needs of society.

A trend of the late 1960s and 1970s was for faculty and students to be appointed to boards of trustees. When students and faculty serve on the board of their own college or university, the potential exists for their thoughts and actions to be determined more by their self-interests than the overall purposes of the institution. This is quite apparent in the circumstance in which a faculty member of a board may be required to vote on a faculty collective bargaining contract, or when a student member of a board must vote on a fee or tuition increase.[4] Because of situations such as these, the ultimate authority for what happens in colleges and universities, like that of any service or instrumental organization, cannot be solely within that organization's membership. External influence, representing those the institution serves, must be dominant, for:

> The university does not exist for its faculty, nor even for its students, alone. It is a servant of society, and each of its individual agents, of whatever class or level, is in a sense a servant of the public. Therefore, the university is appropriately governed, in the eyes of the law, by a body of men and women chosen as representatives of the general public. This body—the governing board, constituting a single artificial person—is the university.[5]

It has been stated that departments of colleges and universities have become so autonomous and self-serving that they have lost sight of the overall goals of the institution. They will tell half-truths and resort to any number of devices to maintain autonomy and preserve self-interests. It has also been asserted that this tendency transcends departments and affects approaches at the institutional level. Administrators are thought to be as responsible for this as faculty:

> . . . there is surprising accord between the aspirations and ends sought by the faculty and those sought by administrators, for the reputation of a university is based largely on research and on the range of programs offered, rather than on the education of students and service to society.[6]

It is the obligation of trustees to see that colleges and universities do not sacrifice the education of students and the meeting of societal needs through public service activities because faculty become too involved in esoteric research and other "scholarly" endeavors understood only by colleagues in highly specialized areas and of little or no value to society in general.

This obligation emphasizes the need for *formal* authority to be vested in a legally incorporated board representing diverse interests of outside "publics." *Informally*, the governance of

the college or university, as a service organization, becomes
much more complicated. The situation is far more complicated
than charters or statutes indicate because individuals not represented on the board of control exercise a significant influence.
They include professional associations; accrediting agencies;
collective bargaining groups for faculty, staff members, and
sometimes middle-management personnel; officials of federal,
state, and local government; leaders in business and industry;
private philanthropic foundation decision makers; and the
courts. Other colleges and universities that have become pace-
setters and models also exert an important influence.

Patterns and Trends in Statewide Coordination, Cooperation, and Control

Other influences upon public higher education directly and
private colleges and universities indirectly have been brought
about through statewide systems of control. In public higher
education a distinction is made between *coordinating* and *governing* agencies when statewide control is considered. In states
where *coordinating* agencies exist, individual state universities
and colleges have boards of control as the legal entities responsible for their program, property, finances, and operations.
However, there is a central agency, which coordinates budget
requests and policies, approves new academic programs, and in
many cases maintains a staff that does long-range planning and
conducts research. In situations where central *governing* agencies
function, all state colleges and universities are under the control of one board of trustees or regents. In addition to responsibilities described for coordinating agencies, central governing
boards have the duties carried out by local governing boards
in systems where central coordinating agencies and local governing boards are in operation. This is true because there are no
local governing boards in systems that are centrally governed.[7]

Further distinctions can be made through discussion of: (1)
voluntary associations; (2) advisory coordinating boards; (3)
regulatory coordinating boards; and (4) consolidated governing
boards.

Voluntary associations are the simplest forms of statewide

coordination, and they were in operation during the earlier
phases of cooperation but no longer exist.[8] These associations
for coordination should not be confused with voluntary consortium arrangements among institutions for various program
areas and operations. Voluntary consortia are increasing and
are discussed more extensively in Chapter 7.

Advisory coordinating boards are statutorally established
agencies located in state capitals. These boards, existing in states
that have governing boards for each public institution or groups
of institutions, provide advice and recommendations to the
state government as well as the state colleges and universities,
but they cannot overrule institutional or institutional group
governing boards.[9] Michigan, Washington, California, Minnesota,
Arkansas, Maryland, and Alabama have boards of this nature.
In Michigan and Washington, each four-year public institution
has its own governing board; in California and Minnesota, a
prestigious "flagship" university is governed by one board and
a state university system of several "lesser" institutions is governed by a second board. In Arkansas, Maryland, and Alabama
some public four-year institutions have their own boards while
others are governed by multicampus agencies.[10]

Regulatory coordinating boards have also been established by
statute in states that have single and multicampus governing
boards. However, the laws creating them specify that they have
final authority in certain areas such as approval of budgets or
new programs, even though they cannot overrule institutional
governing boards in other areas.[11] Regulatory boards function
in Missouri, Kentucky, Connecticut, Illinois, Louisiana, New
York, Tennessee, Colorado, Indiana, New Jersey, New Mexico,
Ohio, Oklahoma, Pennsylvania, South Carolina, Texas, and
Virginia. In Missouri eight of nine four-year institutions have
their own governing boards with the University of Missouri
board having authority over four campuses; in Kentucky all
four-year institutions have boards, and the University of Kentucky board governs two-year colleges as well; in Connecticut
each four-year institution has its own board with the board
responsible for the University of Connecticut also governing
five two-year institutions. Illinois has one board for the University of Illinois, one board governing Southern Illinois Uni-

versity, another board governing three four-year units, and a
fourth board which is responsible for five four-year institutions.
Louisiana, New York, and Tennessee have two or more multicampus boards which govern all four-year institutions with
separate arrangements for universities and for state colleges.
All other states with regulatory boards are characterized by
systems having single boards for some four-year institutions
and one board for a number of campuses in other cases.[12]

Consolidated governing boards have been established by law
in some states to govern and coordinate all four-year institutions
through a single board. These states include Arizona, Florida,
Iowa, Kansas, Hawaii, Mississippi, Wisconsin, Idaho, Montana,
Nevada, North Dakota, Rhode Island, West Virginia, Alaska,
Georgia, South Dakota, New Hampshire, Oregon, Wyoming,
and Massachusetts. In North Carolina, Utah, and Maine, there
is a single governing board for all public four-year institutions.
However, in North Carolina and Utah, that central board has
delegated certain powers to individual campus boards, and in
Maine, a separate board exists for the Maine Maritime Academy.[13]

Delaware, Nebraska, and Vermont do not have statutory
coordinating agencies for public higher education at the state
level. Delaware has an individual governing board for each
institution; Nebraska has multicampus governing boards; and
Vermont has a combination of individual and multicampus
boards for public senior institutions.[14]

In considering statewide coordination of community college
operations, it can be said that greater and greater control has
come about at the state level for these institutions as local
communities have been unable to provide adequate financial
support, and more financial responsibility has been assumed
at the state level.

Historically, control and coordination have been heightened
in times of depression and economic growth. The Panic of 1893,
for example, appears to have caused South Dakota to abolish
institutional governing boards and establish the Board of Regents
for Education for the governance and coordination of the
operations of a land-grant college, an "embryonic" university,
a school of mines, and seven normal schools. This was done to
avoid duplication of offerings and unnecessary costs. The Great

Depression, starting in 1929, saw similar consolidation take
place in Oregon (1929), Georgia (1931), Mississippi (1932),
and North Carolina (1933).[15]

In the late 1950s and throughout the 1960s, the rapid growth
of higher education resulted in extensive competition for funds
among various state colleges and universities within the states
which were providing their financial support. State governments
responded by developing agencies and mechanisms for coordination. The agency progression for this coordination through
the 1950s, 1960s, and 1970s has been from voluntary associations
to coordinating bodies to central governing boards. In this progression the combining of coordinating and governing functions
at the state level results in either the long-range planning and
coordinating function being sacrificed because the board spends
most of its time on the management of institutional affairs, or
a situation in which the board neglects the management of
institutional affairs with the result that the local administration
exercises too much power and the needs of the persons the
board represents in society are not being served. This suggests
that the best arrangement for coordinating and governing may
be one characterized by local governing boards and a statewide
regulatory coordinating agency.[16]

Commenting upon the situation of statewide coordination
of higher education in the early 1970s, M. M. Chambers expressed the opinion that there was an "overcentralization" in
the governing of institutions and that state governments were
attempting to place public colleges and universities under the
same controls used for government agencies. Efforts were being
made to subject the policy-making operations of colleges and
universities to procedures determined by such regulatory arms
of government as the departments of finance and administration.[17]
Local boards of trustees were giving way to single statewide
governing boards, and all too frequently consolidation was
being accomplished for political reasons rather than as a result
of well-thought-out planning involving comments and suggestions
from the many interest groups concerned with the future of
higher education.

Consolidation of higher education in Wisconsin seems to
represent some politics, some planning and reasoning, and some

power. The state historically controlled an extensive system
of higher education through two governing boards. The first
board, the University of Wisconsin Board of Regents, was responsible for campuses in Madison, Milwaukee, Green Bay, and
Kenosha, a number of two-year centers, and a cooperative extension (outreach) program. The second board, the State
University Board of Regents, governed former normal school-
emerging state college-state university units at Superior, Stevens
Point, Oshkosh, LaCrosse, Eau Claire, River Falls, Menomonie,
Platteville, and Whitewater. In the 1960s, a coordinating council
was created to bring together the efforts of the two boards. In
his 1971-1973 budget, Governor Patrick J. Lucey eliminated
the coordinating council and the central administrations of the
State University and University of Wisconsin systems. He proposed one board of regents for all institutions of higher education on the grounds that the old systems of governance were
archaic, costly, and promoted rivalries, which were not in the
best interests of tax-paying citizens. He stated that he was
aware that his actions would be opposed by those who had
vested interests in the old system, but he warned that the government of the state might take over direct control if his plan
did not succeed:

> Let me add that if a rational restructuring of higher
> education fails to pass, then we as elected officials
> will be required to take into our own hands the
> review of planning budgeting throughout higher
> education that should ordinarily be the responsibility
> of an effective, consolidated leadership of the
> universities themselves.[18]

Problems Between Boards Responsible for Public Higher Education and State Government

The two boards for higher education in Wisconsin were
merged, avoiding what may have been a strong confrontation
between the governor and those charged with responsibility

for the control of public universities. However, confrontations
have taken place and are taking place between state government officials and higher education boards. For example, in
1975 Governor Arch Moore of West Virginia wanted the state
system of higher education to take over Greenbrier College of
Osteopathic Medicine, but the state Board of Regents rejected
the idea because of the expense that would be involved. Moore
charged that the board had gone outside its area of authority
into a matter which should be decided by the executive and
legislative branches of government. With his support, the legislature voted $425,000 to fund the West Virginia School of
Osteopathic Medicine for the remainder of the 1974-1975 fiscal
year and $1,290,000 for 1975-1976. This enactment was con-
sidered by the Attorney General of West Virginia to be "permissive," not "mandatory." The Board of Regents refused the
financial support it provided, believing money should be appropriated to pay the expenses of West Virginia students attending osteopathic colleges outside the state. The Regents reasoned
that this would cost the taxpayers less than actually supporting
a school within the state, and they expressed the belief that
the state was attempting to support too many medical schools.
Governor Moore said that he and the people of West Virginia
would decide what the state could afford in higher education
and that the Board of Regents was not supposed to make policy
but was to execute administratively policy made by the governor
and the legislature.[19]

The West Virginia School of Osteopathic Medicine was established in an apparent victory for the governor and the legislature. There are other examples of governing board and state
government conflict which have not resulted in such one-sided
victories. Idaho and nineteen other states have uniform administrative procedures acts that apply to the operations of government agencies. Efforts have been made to apply these acts to
the policies and procedures of state-supported institutions of
higher education. In the case of Idaho, administrative procedures
acts (APA) have been in effect for over fifteen years. Under the
provisions of APA, policies and procedures of state government
agencies must be presented through a public notice and a publication of rules, and opportunities must be afforded for hearings

and other aspects of due process. An Idaho state district court
judge ruled that a 1973 prohibition against student possession
and consumption of alcoholic beverages at state universities
was invalid because it had not been adopted through APA
procedures. This issue raised concern on the part of the Idaho
State Board of Education because it had not followed APA
provisions for academic policies and a whole range of other
policies and procedures at state universities.

The issue of whether all public higher education procedures
should meet APA provisions raised an important question in
1977. At that time, Milton Small, the director of the Idaho
educational board voiced the concern that requiring institutions
of higher education to follow APA specifications for all policies
and procedures would remove governance responsibility from
the hands of the constitutionally established board and create
"a kind of statewide participatory democracy." In 1977, Idaho's
educational officials were successful in gaining legislative ex-
emption to APA guidelines for all policy and procedural decisions
on tuition, admissions, personnel management, student activities
and discipline, degree requirements, curriculum, academic
standards, use of physical facilities, and student housing. The
basis for their approach was that APA provisions were not
intended to be applied to internal management of agencies
when public rights were not being affected. Their approach was
consistent with the reasoning behind practices in most of the
twenty states that have APA's. A slight variation exists in South
Dakota where the legislature has enacted laws that exempt the
Board of Regents from APA provisions on student matters, but
not on faculty policies.[20]

A situation in Nebraska provides another example of higher
education governing board and legislative conflict. In 1977
certain legislative enactments were specifically designed to
reduce the power of the Board of Regents in the areas of com-
pensation for university employees, procedures for purchasing
supplies and equipment, and in regulating the use of instituional
facilities. However, the Supreme Court of Nebraska ruled these
laws unconstitutional because the constitution clearly specified
that policy and decision making for the University of Nebraska
was in the hands of the Regents. The Court stated further that

this was necessary to give the University independence through the Regents as its governing agency. While this decision did establish some independence from the legislature, it said that the legislature could become involved in reappropriation of federal funds designated for the University and in the reappropriation of "line item" allocations. If this was a victory for the University, it certainly was not complete in any context. The Court decision gave the legislature grounds for involvement in specific areas of expenditures. Officials of higher education in Nebraska have down-played this decision, which seems to have removed the University from direct control of the legislature. They recognized that the University relies upon the legislature for tax dollar appropriations. Robert G. Simmons, Chairman of the Board of Regents, said the Court ruling helped eliminate "the nuisance factor" or the activities of some officials in the state department of administrative services who had a tendency to become involved in University operations just about every week.[21]

Experience in California provides some other instances of direct legislative involvement in higher educational affairs. The belief on the part of some legislators in 1970 that the University of California was appointing too many professors from outside the California system to tenured positions without an adequate probationary period led to an interesting attempt at influencing the University. These legislators through a joint resolution proposed a new tenure policy, which was taken under advisement by the Regents but not adopted. At approximately the same time, disgust with the actions of faculty protesting the U. S. invasion of Cambodia seems to have caused the Finance Committee of the State Senate to remove a 5 percent cost of living increase from the budget for faculty salaries. In the Assembly, the Ways and Means Committee deleted funds to be used specifically for the support of the Academic Senate of the University of California. The chair of the Ways and Means Committee explained that this action was intended to agitate what he considered to be an obnoxious group of malcontents, which should be able to finance its activities through dues. While some of the reductions imposed by the Ways and Means Committee were altered, this situation does illustrate that government representatives can humble a faculty body which has been considered to be among the most powerful in academic circles. It has been said that the Academic Senate barely survived that year.[22]

In Colorado in 1979, a letter asking legislators for nominations for the presidency of the University of Colorado, resulted in thirty-six legislators inquiring if it was really necessary to have a president. This response raised questions about the cost to the taxpayers of supporting a high-level administrator in this position, since each of the four campuses in the system was already being led by a chancellor. When the Board of Regents of the University of Colorado received this correspondence, its chair replied by saying that a president *would* be appointed and constitutional provisions prohibited the legislature from eliminating the position. The reaction of the thirty-six legislators to this statement was that they were going to give careful consideration to a statute that reduced the influence of the president and decreased the funding for the support of that office.[23]

In the early 1980s in Massachusetts, a revision in the thirty-unit system of higher education has been characterized by direct involvement of the legislature in the governance of higher education. In 1980 the old structures of governance for higher education were discontinued and a new fifteen-person board of regents was established as an all-powerful agency, which could abolish an entire institution through a two-thirds vote and had the authority to allocate funds as it saw fit from a "lump sum" granted by the legislature. It has been contended that legislative leaders, especially the chair of the Senate Ways and Means Committee, Chester G. Atkins, have virtually taken over the control of the governance system of higher education during this transitional period when one board has become supreme and the office of the state education secretary, the statewide coordinating board, and a number of multicampus boards have been abolished. Legislative leaders have denied this controlling involvement, but an important budget officer has stated that the budgetary process will be vital in all decisions on major public policy. This provides another avenue for legislative intervention in higher education. The opinion has also been stated that many legislators will be reluctant to give the Regents the full authority legislation grants because that power may be politically damaging to those legislators in their home districts.[24]

The relationship between the people most directly responsible for higher education, boards and college and university officials, is an uneasy one. John Millett discusses this situation when he refers to the role of the Ohio Board of Regents. He states that the position of the Regents is at a midpoint between the executive and legislative branches of state government on one side and the state universities on the other end. Expectations are conflicting, since the state universities believe the Regents should be their advocate and convince the governor and the legislature to go along with their wishes. The governor and the legislature expect the Regents to:

> . . . keep the universities in their place, to cool their
> aspirations, to curtail their appropriation requests,
> to supervise their operations, and to bring account-
> ability into the realm of their activities.[25]

Millett believes the role of the Regents is to help the state government in determining and voicing "the politically desirable and reasonable policies concerning higher education." The Regents are to insure that higher education is responsible to the needs of society at the same time that it strives for "a maximum degree of institutional autonomy" for each of the units within the system.[26]

Board Responsibilities

Millett's position relates to the responsibilities of statewide coordinating agencies. When these agencies also have the authority to govern, they have many of the same responsibilities as single campus or multiple-campus governing boards. Boards of trustees are responsible for all that takes place at the institutions for which statutes or charters hold them accountable. However, they are policy makers and not managers. They must see that institutions are managed efficiently, effectively, and in keeping with the purposes of the institutions. They are to appoint,

evaluate, and remove, when they believe necessary, the president
of the institution. They oversee the essential function of the
institution, hold the title to institutional property, supervise
the financial activities of the institution, serve as a court of last
resort, and maintain the charter and revise it when such action
is appropriate.[27] Financial responsibilities include the management of institutional endowment and the investment of funds.

Another way to express board responsibilities is to say that
they hold college or university educational programs and services, and the institutional material and human resources necessary to accomplish program and service goals, in "trust." Financial and physical assets are held in trust and must be used in
the interests of certain beneficiaries:

> Beneficiaries can be the general public (open admis-
> sions) or those who qualify on academic, religious
> or residential criteria; they can be business and in-
> dustry or the general welfare, as in the case of
> agricultural extension programs of land-grant col-
> leges or research programs of major universities.[28]

Board responsibility for the accomplishment of the educational
mission of the institution means that it must see that a statement
of mission is written by the administration, but usually involving
faculty. It is the duty of the board to interpret this statement to
institutional constituencies, to review it from time to time, and
to see that changes are made to reflect developments in society
in general when a change in mission is desired because of these
developments. Board members should see that the interests of
the governor, legislators, and a central board of regents are considered in mission statements in the case of publicly assisted
or supported colleges and universities.[29]

Since missions are accomplished through certain short-range
and long-range plans relating to programs, activities, and resources, boards have final approval over long-range plans. Institutional administrators and staffs are directly responsible
for plans, but boards must see that they do it. Once boards
approve mission statements and the plans to accomplish objectives specified in these statements, they continuously oversee

educational programs and services and ensure that financial
solvency is maintained. Another important aspect of oversight
responsibility of boards is to see that insitutional independence
is preserved. This is a most difficult task in reality because
special interest groups, especially those who provide substantial
financial support, will exert pressure on colleges and universities
to promote programs and services that benefit or are supportive
of those interests, or at least the special interest groups will
oppose activities that threaten their interests.[30]

Trustees have an important obligation to see that instituional
education programs and services reflect the needs of those
constituencies that mission statements say these programs and
services are to serve. It is in the consideration of this area that
distinctions between the roles of boards serving public and
private colleges and universities can be drawn. The boards for
public institutions are, in essence, substitutes for the power of
governors, assemblies, and senates. These boards develop rules,
regulations, and policies for the conduct of operations of
public institutions which would otherwise be done by legislative
and executive branches of state government. Direct involvement
of governors and legislatures has been thought to be undesirable
because it causes institutions of higher education to become too
political or unprotected from the whims of the politicians. Boards
for public colleges and universities were established to provide
insulation from the political process. While boards represent the
public interest, they are one step removed from politics in those
states where their members are appointed rather than elected.
It should be noted that this theory may not apply in those states
in which board members are elected through popular vote.[31]

Private institution boards are different because their members
are supposed to view policies, programs, and procedures from
a broad societal rather than political perspective. The theory
is that they rely on their personal observations and experiences
and moral and ethical princples to determine what programs,
policies, and plans are in the best interests of society as a whole.
Millett refers to the basis of trusteeship in private colleges and
universities as being a "collective social conscience."[32] It might
be argued that the reasoning that Millett presents for the role
of the private college board of trustees members represents a

real "pie-in-the-sky" dream because few persons have the perspective to represent all of society. In fact, most private college board members have a distinct corporate business or professional perspective. If this perspective is appropriate for a collective social conscience, it can be said that these trustees do serve the interests of society in general. That these interests are representative of society as a whole is debatable, to say the very least. However, the reality is that this seems to be the premise upon which private board of control membership is based.

Other differences exist between public and private boards. Size and method of appointment indicate distinctions. Public boards usually consist of an average of nine members appointed by the governor for staggered office terms ranging frequently from seven to fifteen years. These appointments generally are subject to ratification by a state legislative body. In some instances, usually in the situation of statewide coordinating boards, some or all members may be elected by the citizenry. In the case of private boards, membership is self-perpetuating, frequently for life or until a specified retirement age has been reached. Private boards may number from twenty-five to fifty members. If the private college or university has some relationship with a church, that denominational body may appoint some members. It should be added that alumni may elect some members to private institutional boards; however, this membership is usually a minority of the total board.[33]

The large size of private college or university boards makes the functioning of committees especially important for those institutions although a significant role is also played by board committees at public institutions. Committees carry such titles as: (1) personnel committee (faculty and student affairs); (2) finance committee; (3) executive committee, especially important for the large private institution board, which can not meet frequently enough to consider many problems that demand more immediate attention; (4) curriculum committee; and (5) buildings and grounds committee. Other names for standing committees might include: (1) audit committee; (2) budget committee; (3) development committee; (4) investment committee; (5) honorary degrees committee; (6) nominations committee; and (7) library committee. The use of board committees

is valuable because it enables the board to accomplish a greater
amount of business than it can when it meets as a committee
of the whole, it affords an opportunity for board members to
become better educated in terms of problems encountered by
the institution because it gives them more contact, it allows
for a more efficient use of the special interests and talents of
individual board members, and it facilitates involvement of
local members who are more readily available when the total
board consists of members from widely spread geographical
regions. The committee system also provides for a better screen-
ing and examination of business that needs to go before the
total board for action.[34]

In recent years, more use has been made of ad hoc committees
and task forces consisting not only of trustees, but of administrators, alumni, staff, faculty, and students. Trustee service on
such committees can provide significant opportunity for direct
contact with faculty, staff, alumni, students, and other interest
groups that are concerned with the institution. Cleveland State
University was responsible for a pioneering effort in this area
in 1969 when three members of the University's board of trustees
participated in a weekend retreat sponsored by the institution's
student government. Traditionally, the purpose of this retreat
had been to provide an opportunity for administrators, faculty,
and student leaders to discuss major problems confronting the
University and to "brainstorm" some possible solutions. Involvement of the three board members of the Cleveland State University Board of Trustees Student Affairs Committee—a prominent physician, a retired executive from the telephone company,
and a local judge—provided an added dimension for understanding and acceptance among persons who had a vital interest in
the institution's future.

Characteristics of Governing Boards Today

Understanding the perspectives of the many persons who have
an interest in higher education is a difficult task which requires
that board members have some special strengths and insights.
Their backgrounds and characteristics are important. In 1977,
three studies conducted under the auspices of the Association

of Governing Boards of Universities and Colleges, the Office
for the Advancement of Public Negro Colleges, and the American
Association of Community and Junior Colleges that presented
the backgrounds and characteristics of board members were
reported. The information on sex and race of members has
already been given in the first chapter. That chapter, concerning
special influences on higher education, also indicated percentages
of board members who were business executives, clergy, lawyers,
and physicians and dentists. These studies indicated that 47,138
trustees and regents served on 2,314 boards governing 3,037
campuses in the United States. Boards governing more than one
institution were much more common for public institutions: 1,544
boards governed 1,588 private institutions; 770 boards governed
1,448 public colleges and universities with 164 multi-campus
boards governing 886 public institutions; and 40,225 board
members out of the total of 47,138 served private colleges and
universities. The average private college or university board has
twenty-eight members while nine is the average for public boards.[35]

An occupational analysis revealed, in addition to percentages
reported in the chapter on special influences, the following
occupations of board members and the percentages of persons
in those occupations:

Other professionals	1.1 percent
College administrators	5.9 percent
College faculty members	3.3 percent
College students	1.0 percent
Elementary or secondary school teachers or administrators	2.9 percent
Other educational workers	0.7 percent
Executives of nonprofit organizations	4.1 percent
Homemakers	5.0 percent
Farmers	1.3 percent
Retired persons	9.1 percent
Others	7.1 percent

The Association of Governing Boards of Universities and Colleges
study consisted of national projections based upon data on

449 boards governing 1,021 institutions. These data revealed
that the typical board member was a white male in his fifties.
Board members for public institutions tended to be younger
than those at private colleges and universities. More board
members at private institutions were corporate presidents than
at public colleges and universities. The Office for the Advancement of Public Negro Colleges study indicated that there were
171 trustees for 34 institutions, 62 percent of board members
were white, 80 percent were fifty years of age or older, 83
percent were males, 93 percent were college graduates, and of
the fifteen respondents who were board chairs, all agreed that
obtaining state tax dollar subsidies was a major task. Twelve of
the fifteen chairs believed that part of their responsibility was
raising funds from nonstate sources. When chairs were asked
if their states had provided special funds within the past five
years to compensate for earlier discrimination, seven said yes,
seven said no, and one did not reply. The survey conducted by
the American Association of Community and Junior Colleges
(443 public and 92 private two-year colleges) asked institutional
chief executives and board chairs to respond to certain questions.
These responses indicated the belief that more time should be
spent on long-range planning and evaluation of educational
programs. It was also agreed that budgets and finances were
major issues, but that only a moderate amount of board time
should be spent on them. Major issues were ranked: (1) funding
formulas; (2) capital planning; (3) program cutbacks; (4) enrollment projections; and (5) long-range planning.[36]

The backgrounds and interests of board members have an
influence on their involvement in the governance of colleges
and universities. Areas of involvement have remained relatively
constant over the years at four-year institutions. Since most
trustees continue to have backgrounds in business, they prefer
activities in which they have experience, mainly those related
to financial, physical plant, public relations, and political
matters.[37]

Members of boards face an interesting dilemma. While they
themselves have been charged with the awesome task of balancing and synthesizing the many special interests impinging on
higher education, the survival of both public and private higher

education in the future may require recognition that boards are
a special interest group which needs to become the collective
advocate of *all* higher education, not just the specific institutions
they serve officially. Richart T. Ingram expresses the belief that
the role of trustees will change to the extent that they actually
constitute a special interest group rather than functioning as
an agency for balancing the interests of other special interest
groups. He refers to the emergence of fifteen state trustee associations promoted most vigorously by community colleges,
which he claims have boards that are more enthusiastic concerning political activity than boards representing other colleges
and universities. Ingram's position advocates greater support
of statewide associations similar in make-up to that of the
Association of Governing Boards of Universities and Colleges.[38]
The implications of this position deserve careful consideration.
If board members form associations at state, regional, and
national levels, and if these associations become the major
determinants of policy, the needs and interests of specific communities become secondary. This approach should be kept in
mind as a negative influence when the area of public service is
discussed in Chapter 8 of this book. If the membership of
college and university boards of trustees is predominantly
corporate power oriented, as the literature suggests, what
happens to the interests and needs of local communities and
segments of society whose interests are not served when the
corporations prevail?

Summary

The background and experience of any individual or group
determines how that individual or group will view the goals
and programs of colleges and universities. In the earliest history
of the United States persons in positions of power (the courts)
considered colleges to have the status of private corporations
relatively immune from any outside interference. Presidents
emerged as key figures in determining the direction of higher
education because frontier conditions required legal responsibility to be placed in the hands of nonresident trustees. While
presidents emerged as strong figures, other conditions balanced

their powers. "Absentee" or nonresident boards maintained their power to appoint and remove presidents, faculty influence was maintained from the English tradition, and certain groups outside the formal structure of higher educational institutions emerged as important influences on policy and programs. A public commitment to education meant that tax dollars spent for higher education should be in the direction of the interests of citizens; state legislators and representatives of the executive branch of government gained inroads in college and university policymaking and program development because of their responsibility to the public.

The outcome of all of this for higher education in America has been that many people have a stake in the endeavors of colleges and universities. Checks and balances are needed to insure that this diversity of interest is reflected in educational programs and services. Governmental representatives must be involved, the power of corporations must be taken into account (for better or worse, Calvin Coolidge's observation that the business of this country is business must be recognized), and every effort should be exerted to recognize local and individual interest. This has been, and will continue to be, a most difficult assignment for any person who serves as a board of trustees member.

Notes

1. John S. Brubacher and Willis Rudy, *Higher Education in Transition: A History of American Colleges and Universities, 1636-1976*, 3d. ed. rev. and enl. (New York: Harper and Row, 1976), pp. 409-410.

2. George W. Angell and Edward P. Kelley, Jr., "Responding to Unionism," in *Handbook of College and University Trusteeship*, ed. Richard T. Ingram (San Francisco: Jossey-Bass, 1980), p. 263.

3. William H. Cowley, "An Overview of American Colleges and Universities, Parts I-IV," mimeographed (Stanford, California: Stanford University, 1960), pp. 103-104.

4. Malcolm G. Scully, "Bar Professors, Students, as Trustees of Their Own Colleges, Panel Urges," *Chronicle of Higher Education*, July 28, 1980, p. 4.

5. Merritt M. Chambers, "Who is the University?" *Journal of Higher Education* 30 (June 1959): 324.

6. Paul L. Dressel, F. Craig Johnson, and Philip M. Marcus, *The Confidence Crisis* (San Francisco: Jossey-Bass, 1970), p. 232.

7. Cowley, "An Overview of American Colleges and Universities, Parts I-IV," p. 118.

8. Kenneth P. Mortimer and T. R. McConnell, *Sharing Authority Effectively* (San Francisco: Jossey-Bass, 1978), p. 219.

9. Ibid.

10. Carnegie Foundation for the Advancement of Teaching, *The States and Higher Education: A Proud Past and a Vital Future* (New York: Carnegie Foundation for the Advancement of Teaching, 1976), pp. 55-57.

11. Mortimer and McConnell, *Sharing Authority Effectively*, p. 219.

12. Carnegie Foundation for the Advancement of Teaching, *The States and Higher Education: A Proud Past and a Vital Future*, pp. 55-57, 61.

13. Ibid., pp. 57-59.

14. Ibid., pp. 55-56.

15. Merritt M. Chambers, *Higher Education: Who Pays? Who Gains?* (Danville, Illinois: Interstate Printers and Publishers, 1968), pp. 207-208.

16. James L. Miller, Address at Kent State University, Kent, Ohio, April 3, 1975.

17. Merritt M. Chambers, *Higher Education and State Governments, 1970-1975* (Danville, Illinois: Interstate Printers and Publishers, 1974), p. 5.

18. Patrick J. Lucey, *Governor's Budget Message, 1971-1973, Part II: Policy Changes and Cost Reductions* (Madison, Wisconsin: State of Wisconsin, undated), pp. 2-4.

19. "Governor vs. Regents," *Chronicle of Higher Education*, May 27, 1975, p. 4.

20. Robert L. Jacobson, "Court Ruling Seen Threat to Idaho Board's Authority," *Chronicle of Higher Education*, July 25, 1977, p. 9.

21. Robert L. Jacobson, "In Nebraska, a Court Decision has Upheld the Legal Autonomy of the State University, but Savvy Officials say They Won't Forget it's the Legislature That Holds the Purse Strings," *Chronicle of Higher Education*, September 6, 1977, pp. 7-8.

22. Robert M. O'Neil, "Law and Higher Education in California," in *Governing Academic Organizations*, ed. Gary L. Riley and J. Victor Baldridge (Berkeley, California: McCutcheon Publishing, 1977), pp. 176-177.

23. Robert L. Jacobson, "Colorado Legislators Ask: Is President Needed?" *Chronicle of Higher Education*, July 23, 1979, p. 2.

24. Robert L. Jacobson, "Massachusetts System Thrown Into Turmoil by a Wrangle Over Finances and Governance," *Chronicle of Higher Education*, February 10, 1982, pp. 1, 4-5.

25. John D. Millett, *Politics and Higher Education* (University, Alabama: University of Alabama Press, 1975), p. 120.

26. Ibid., pp. 120-121.

27. Morton A. Rauh, *College and University Trusteeship* (Yellow Springs, Ohio: Antioch Press, 1959), pp. 17-19.

28. John W. Nason, "Responsibilities of the Governing Board," in *Handbook of College and University Trusteeship*, ed. Richards T. Ingram (San Francisco: Jossey-Bass, 1980), p. 27.

29. Ibid., pp. 33-35.

30. Ibid., pp. 35-40.

31. John D. Millett, "Similarities and Differences Among Universities of the United States," in *The University as an Organization*, ed. James A. Perkins (New York: McGraw-Hill, 1973), pp. 51-52.

32. Ibid., p. 51.

33. Ibid.

34. Morton A. Rauh, "Internal Organization of the Board," in *The University as an Organization*, ed. James A. Perkins (New York: McGraw-Hill, 1973), p. 234.

35. Jack Magarrell, "Who Controls the Universities?" *Chronicle of Higher Education*, September 6, 1977, p. 7.

36. Ibid.

37. John J. Corson, "Participating in Policy Making and Management," in *Handbook of College and University Trusteeship*, ed. Richard T. Ingram (San Francisco: Jossey-Bass, 1980), p. 110.

38. Richard T. Ingram, "Toward Effective Trusteeship in the Eighties," in *Handbook of College and University Trusteeship*, ed. Richard T. Ingram (San Francisco: Jossey-Bass, 1980), pp. 10-11.

3

INTERNAL GOVERNANCE

All administrators, whether they serve governments, businesses, or colleges and universities, are responsible for certain functions and encounter some general problems in performing their duties. While leadership styles and orientations may differ from person to person, overall tasks of administrators always concern putting together human resources (people with varied interests and talents) and material resources (money, physical facilities, and equipment) to accomplish a particular objective or set of objectives.

Management in General

Leaders must make plans for their groups, organizations, or institutions based on purposes and goals. Resources must be organized into units or components and administrators are responsible for coordinating the operation of these parts. A vital aspect of organizing and coordinating involves selecting the "right" unit leaders, placing them in charge of components, and delegating responsibility to them. The administrator has the overall task of communicating and explaining all information related to goals, plans, resources, specific objectives, and performance of persons and programs when that information is necessary for the effective and efficient operation of the organization.

Coordinating, communicating, and explaining are required to maintain control over the direction in which the organization is moving and to make changes in both personnel and programs when objectives are not being accomplished. Critical and constructive evaluation is absolutely essential in the achievement of the latter. Just as essential in control is the need for the administrator to make decisions at important points in the life and activities of the organization. Whether it is in planning, organizing, coordinating, communicating, controlling, or evaluating, the administrator who is responsible must make decisions.[1] Ideally these decisions are made on the best information available, as many facts as possible are taken into account, and people who have the best knowledge of the situation are involved in the decision-making process.

How an administrator works with people in an organization, whether in day-to-day routine contacts or in crisis situations requiring major decisions, depends upon his or her values and beliefs concerning the human individual, human groups, and work. A number of theories and practices have emerged concerning values and beliefs in this area, but three major movements in the history of management in American society have had an important influence.

Scientific management gained widespread recognition as an appropriate approach in the latter part of the nineteenth and the early part of the twentieth century. This orientation, based on the thinking of economist Adam Smith and administrative scientist Frederick Taylor, focused on people's economic nature. Concentration was upon work specialization and wage analysis with major consideration being given to doing a particular task at a fair wage, and the principal assumption was that money was the main motivator for behavior.[2]

The *human relations movement* came about because industrial psychologists found in the 1920s and 1930s that people had strong psychological needs, which might be classified as recognition, security, accomplishment, and involvement. The research conducted by Elton Mayo at the Western Electric Company and its introduction of the "Hawthorne Effect" are well known and have influenced this movement. This movement has also been characterized by awareness that informal power structures and influences have existed within formal organizations. The human relations movement recognized that managerial effectiveness relates directly to the consideration of and sensitivity to diversification and variation in human needs. This movement reached its peak in the 1950s and seemed to decline because human relations techniques were hard to measure empirically in a tough profit-and-loss system.[3]

Industrial humanism seems to be the current theoretical trend in progressive management philosophy. Douglas McGregor, Chris Argyris, and Rensis Likert have been the "poet laureates" of this school, and the work of Abraham Maslow has formed the foundation for this approach. In considering industrial humanism as the high water mark in management philosophy to date, it should be emphasized that Maslow's thesis on human development has been that basic philosophical and social-psychological needs for safety and security must be met before any consideration can be given to higher social and ego needs such as "self-actualization," in which a person's activities, interests, and special talents can be used to the fullest extent to bring about change and creative applications. While Maslow's approach can be criticized on the grounds that stress and discomfort can produce creative action for survival, it can be said that believing a worker wants to be self-actualizing will help a manager facilitate the development of a trust relationship with that employee. Part of this approach is the belief that when a person is given a chance to become involved—utilizing talents, imagination, and interests—the end product will be better because it provides for greater worker satisfaction and pleasure. It should also be emphasized in the industrial humanism approach that trust and participation are crucial in management because they can provide for a leader's flexibility in allowing for many varieties of participation opportunities for employees, according to the individual needs and interests of those employees. This management flexibility permits a blending of individual goals with overall organization objectives.[4]

The values and beliefs of college and university administrators concerning people in work situations can follow the basic lines of scientific management, the human relations movement, or industrial humanism. These administrators can also fall heir to many of the problems encountered by leaders in business and industrial organizations. Opportunities to exert leadership and

provide new directions can become swallowed up in vast bureaucratic organizations with a complicated hierarchial chain
of command, divisions of labor, task specialization, spans of
control,[5] and a machine-like mentality in which functions,
structures, and positions become more important than goals,
people, and creative ideas. Rules and routines replace decisions
that are based upon needs for change and innovation.

The Position of the College President

Administrators in higher education are also subject to having
their egos inflated because of the positions of authority in
which they find themselves. Power simply does something to
people whether this power comes through an important position in business, government, or education. Many leaders tend
to think that they have some special ability to come up with
the right answers in spite of any advice and suggestions they
might receive from their subordinates. Regardless of the experience they might have and the years in which they have
studied administration, this affliction strikes them. In higher
education it may come about because presidents are the only
persons in the system to have a total perspective on the entire
institution. They have access to information and understandings
of this information as it influences instructional, public service,
and research programs in a way that no other executive officer
of the institution has, because the "big picture" is clearly the
presidents' responsibility. This places them in a position in
which they have no equals within the structure of the institution.
This special circumstance of the college or university president
must be recognized for the problems it can create for the
individual human being in that position and its implications
for the direction of higher education, past, present, and future.
Most chief executive officers in business and government face
similar problems, but college and university presidents are com-
pelled to recognize the somewhat unique position of faculty.
Most administrative areas in higher education can be effectively,
efficiently, and humanely managed through an honest application of industrial humanism. However, specific consideration

of leadership with respect to faculty and academic departments requires examination of the social-political context and traditional practices relevant to colleges and universities.

Colleges and universities are like all other organizations to the extent that individuals within these organizations play different roles and occupy different positions. These roles and positions determine different behavior, and they have a certain status attached to them. Certain roles have greater prestige and esteem than others depending upon the perspective, interests, and objectives of the particular faculty member who is considering those roles. In colleges and universities, roles and statuses have special significance for policy and decision-making processes. Frequently, participants in a debate over goals, policy, or any other aspect of organizational programs and procedures are more concerned with their status and self-esteem than they are with actual content, direction, or outcome of the issue being considered. As long as they look good as faculty leaders and their positions of authority have been preserved, the outcome is of little significance.[6]

A realistic appraisal of the collegiate environment requires the dispelling of some myths about colleges and universities as communities. Sociologist Robert M. MacIver made a distinction many years ago between a community and an association. This distinction has particular relevance for an understanding of the nature of the climate of colleges and universities and the rejection of certain claims that have been made for colleges and universities as "true" communities. Implied in MacIver's thesis is that people become members of communities because they wish to share common experiences in a neighborhood, village, or town. They desire a common life, and the basis for the establishment of this relationship is usually voluntary. Exchanges among members of communities are usually casual, informal, and valued intrinsically for what they are and not for what they will produce. On the other hand, people become members of associations because they can attain certain goals or achieve common interests through such an affiliation. In the context of MacIver's thesis, the end is significant in this relationship, not the process, as in the case of communities. Many of the idealistic notions about "communities of scholars" therefore can be discarded because colleges and universities are associations and not communities.[7]

A focus on ends rather than processes and relationships permits an authentic consideration of what various individuals and groups expect as a result of the association, and it allows for an accommodation of special interest and for the establishment of a division of labor. Division of labor is a characteristic of just about every organization of any magnitude in a complex society. It recognizes that the broad goals of an association can take into account the special interests, talents, and objectives of persons who become affiliated with that organization. It allows for a consideration of personal as well as organizational goals. Colleges and universities have broad educational goals to which all members of those associations adhere, but the specific interpretation of those goals depends upon the perspectives of individuals and groups within the association. Previous discussion of Hume's theory of knowledge is important here because it relates to the manner in which experience, habit, feeling, and belief influence perception and judgment. As human individuals perceive knowledge, truth, and reality on the basis of their individual needs, experiences, and interests, those who have common needs, interests, and experiences have a group perspective concerning the goals of an organization. Within a college or university, a number of different group perspectives on organizational goals are possible. It might even be said that these group perspectives constitute "factions" within an organization. This relates to earlier discussion of factions within the general public and the significance of special interest groups in American society.

The Position of the Faculty

The position of the faculty as a special interest group can be discussed to illustrate this point. Faculty members differ quite clearly from presidents in terms of their expectations for their colleges and universities. There is evidence that faculty members place a premium on academic freedom and the pursuit of truth, scholarly research, attaining prestige for graduate programs, rewarding faculty on the basis of contributions to their disciplines

and professions (rather than contributions to the institution),
and pure research for the advancement of knowledge in general.
College and university presidents view the most important goals
of higher education to be protecting academic freedom, protecting and preserving institutional prestige, protecting and preserving program quality, and maintaining financial contributors'
confidence.[8]

While there are similarities between the rating of goals of
colleges and universities by faculty and presidents, the latter
view goals from an overall or "big picture" perspective and the
former consider goals from a special interest vantage point,
which has been complicated by a number of circumstances.
Unlike the president who gains recognition from, and is judged
on the basis of, success or failure of the institution, the faculty
member's highest level of recognition comes through achievements in research and writing in a particular field of study. The
emphasis may be somewhat different in the community college
or small liberal arts institutions where teaching may be more
important, but research and publication and recognition in a
particular academic discipline are increasing in significance
even at these colleges. The interests of a faculty member may
be more attuned to those of colleagues outside the department
and the institution. Specialization has caused an isolation of
the faculty member from other persons and groups within the
college or university he or she serves because the complex nature
of society and scientific and technological advancement require
greater in-depth knowledge in increasingly more precise and
defined areas. Therefore, research and scholarship in specialized
areas cause the faculty member to relate more to colleagues at
other institutions who share that specialization and understand
its significance.[9] If a faculty member's rewards and satisfactions
stem from research, writing, and communicating and collabor-
ating with persons from outside the institution, that faculty
member's principal concern with the policies and operations
of the institution are limited to insuring that he or she has the
freedom and capacity to carry out these activities and receive
recognition and rewards for them.

With research and writing as major concerns, the faculty
member will become involved in the consideration and

development of institutional policies and practices on a highly selective and biased basis. Admissions standards and student aid will be important because they relate to recruitment and retention of quality students who can assist in research. Equipment, supplies, and library expenditures are significant because they support quality research. Travel funds can be major issues for the faculty member because they are necessary for national involvement in scholarly activity or research with colleagues outside the institution. Teaching loads and committee assignments are crucial considerations for faculty because they might impinge upon research and writing time. Salary schedules and increases and promotion standards are important, as they influence a faculty member's standing and prestige with colleagues. Academic freedom and tenure, interpreted as security to hold a faculty position when taking a highly controversial position, become especially important to a faculty member whose political views have caused extreme embarrassment to the administration.

Further biases in the faculty member's approach to policy and decision making in the institution derive from other situations. In addition to research and scholarly writing, the faculty member is expected to serve the college or university as a member of committees and councils. The faculty member is also expected to become involved in public service activities in which he or she applies his or her special knowledge to the solution of problems experienced by some agency or organization in the community. Frequently the reward system is unclear as to just how much time and effort should be committed to each of these areas of activity. Balancing these expectations and participation in scholarly pursuits outside the institution gives the faculty member a special perspective concerning the institution and its administrative leaders. These circumstances tend to place the faculty member in a role that is adversary to that of the administration. Competition for scarce funds may also cause a further division among faculty in various schools and departments. Factions develop within faculty ranks as a result, and the situation can become extremely political.

These developments have taken place in an environment characterized by traditions going back to the Middle Ages when European faculty guilds were the primary policy-making bodies for universities. The tradition of faculty involvement in institutional governance has varied among colleges and universities, usually relating to founding date and prestige. Ivy League institutions, and such educational leaders as Stanford University, the University of Chicago, Johns Hopkins University and the Universities of California, Wisconsin, Michigan, and Minnesota, for example, have had greater faculty involvement than state universities that evolved from a normal school-teachers' college foundation of authoritarian administrative rule similar to that of public school systems. Community colleges emerging from those systems have tended to experience the same governance.

The involvement of faculty in policy determination has been more through tradition than on the basis of legal authorization. Faculty councils and senates are advisory to presidents, for the most part, and the best way for them to have an influence has been constant involvement in a continual prodding of the administration and a perpetual raising of voices. For the faculty, any impact has come more through relentless participation and "squeeky wheelism" than through statutory authority. When their participation is infrequent and selective because of special interests in the educational enterprise and their commitment to research and scholarly activity, that influence is weakened and will tend to fade away.[10]

The Political Nature of Colleges and Universities

It may be that the special interest group position of the faculty and the increased awareness of the impact of politics in times of decreasing financial support have caused the development of collective bargaining arrangements on college campuses. Collective bargaining groups, while they have experienced the no growth-decline syndrome of most unions in the economic hard times of the 1980s, do provide a legal contract basis for faculty participation as an alternative to the "hit-and-run" involvement through faculty councils and senates. Collective bargaining may actually be a more appropriate vehicle for faculty involvement. It recognizes the political model of college and university governance presented by J. Victor Baldridge several years ago. He rejected the revered collegial model, which reflected the European faculty guild ideal, and he questioned the applicability of the bureaucratic model taken from administration in government and industry. In the place of these models, he recommended one that takes into account conflict and special interests among internal constituencies of the college or university. Baldridge argued that bureaucratic models may cover structure, formal relationship, power, and authority in the higher educational setting, but that they do not provide appropriate treatment for change, process, tradition, informal power, and other dynamics of the functioning university.[11]

With respect to collegial models, the most significant statement may be that they have been largely a myth in American higher education with perhaps the exception of some academic departments within larger academic complexes and certain liberal arts colleges with strong religious affiliations and special senses of community.

The political model is based on conflict theory, community power theory, and interest group theory. It recognizes different subgoals for subsystems and differing interpretation of major goals and specific interest (subsystem) needs and desires. It stresses the significance of the informal power structure and allows for an awareness that change and survival come about through compromises, trade-offs, and synthesis among special interest groups. Above all, it seems to accept the notion that faculty members have special interests and needs for survival, which transcend the broad, philosophical, and noble goal of what is best for the student and the nation. In the 1980s it seems clearly ridiculous to accept the idea that faculty members will be so altruistic, benevolent, and wise that they always do what is best for the student and the advancement of knowledge. Colleges and universities in the United States exist in a social-political environment which pits one socioeconomic-political group against another. Also, specialization, the complexity of large organizations, and technological developments have influenced higher education and have meant that professional management is necessary, if colleges and universities are to sruvive in the United States. Faculty collective bargaining seems to reflect these realities. The acceptance of special interests in higher education means that collective negotiations on the part of faculty members are here and will remain in some form or another. Faculty unions may be "disaffiliated" through votes of the idealistic who find the concept of unionization distasteful, but the functions of the unions will be taken on by faculty senates and councils in the years to come as covert if not overt attention is given to the nature of special interest groups in higher education.

The Academic Department

Whether faculty participation in institutional governance is realized through union contract or the older faculty senate or council structure or perhaps through both, the position of the academic department and its administration are crucial. The academic department is the central unit for the performance of instruction, conducting research, and the delivery of service, and the problems resulting from its development of too much autonomy have been discussed in the chapter on external governance.

However, it is at the departmental level that main concerns of faculty members can be addressed and advanced to college and university administrators, councils, and committees. Ideally, it is here that faculty can initiate formal procedures in the originating, discussing, and recommending of educational policies in the areas of current operations of the institutions, and long-range policy and planning in terms of admission policies and standards, degree requirements, establishment and maintenance of new educational and research units, institutional size, auxiliary agencies of a cultural nature, and issues related to faculty status and privileges. Matters pertaining to instruction, research, and public service can be discussed as can the overall welfare of the institution from the perspectives of particular departments.[12] If there is any semblance of collegiality in which respected friends freely exchange ideas in open debate where knowledge and not position of power is foremost, it would probably be at the departmental level.

Because of this tradition, the administrative position that appears to be of particular significance to the faculty member is that of the chair or head of the academic department. Although the faculty member realizes that the dean, vice president, or president exercises more power, he or she appreciates that entree to administrative channels is through the departmental chair. The conflict between administration and faculty, which started in America in colonial times, is least acute at the departmental level. While the chair represents the administration, he or she is still regarded as a colleague by most faculty members in the department.[13] He or she is believed to have an understanding of the faculty perspective because the chair usually teaches at least one course per term, is expected to pursue research and publication interests, and is a bona fide member of the discipline of the department. A chair usually does not gain his or her position without substantial support from the faculty of the department, even though the final selection is made by the dean. However, the position of authority of the chair can vary from institution to institution and college to college. In some cases, the position has been more or less neutralized through the union contract or detailed procedures and policies related to a specific committee structure and faculty governance. On the other hand, leadership for the department might be exercised by an autocratic head. The chair in other instances may be no more than a glorified clerk who is there to serve the senior professors. Whatever the authority, the chair is frequently caught in the middle of conflicts resulting from differences in interest and opinion of the dean as opposed to those of department faculty.

The success of the chair depends upon his or her ability to relate to and maintain the confidence of both the dean and department members in these conflicts and in other situations. Success also coincides with the chair's capacity to cooperate, compromise, and sometimes triumph in interaction with other chairs. Adroitness in dealing with students, faculty committees, alumni, practitioners in the field (in the case of professional departments), and accrediting associations is a further requirement for success. Major responsibilities of the chair include: (1) maintaining communication with all of the persons and groups both internal and external to the institution who have a direct influence on the department's activities; (2) developing class and teaching schedules; (3) preparing the budget and

supervising financial expenditures; (4) evaluating faculty (important for promotion, tenure, and salary increases); (5) developing and evaluating the curriculum; (6) office management;
(7) recruitment and professional development of faculty members; (8) chairing meetings, appointing necessary committees,
and long-range planning; and (9) recruitment of students.[14] In
larger departments, the roles of the chairs are highly similar
to those of deans.

Student Participation in Policy and Decision Making

When the interests, needs, and roles of faculty members are
considered as they relate to participation in the governance
of colleges and universities, it becomes quite apparent that the
management of institutions of higher education has some basic
differences from that of business and governmental organizations.
The status of the student has also been responsible for some
special circumstances. Arguments have been presented by many
educators over the years for the involvement of students in
governance for both organizational development and educational
reasons. Students themselves have demanded participation with
these demands ebbing and flowing on the basis of broader social,
political, and economic conditions.

Whether the times are responsible for a passive, vocationally
oriented student body or a situation in which college and
university campuses are characterized by the presence of activ-
ist students in quest of social and political justice and human
rights, involvement of students in institutional governance is
sound developmental and educational policy. Opportunities for
this participation should exist on a continuous basis regardless
of student climate. Unfortunately many college and university
administrators today have eliminated students from the policy
and decision-making processes and have assumed authoritarian
roles because action can be taken more quickly and efficiently
this way and students are not demanding the involvement they
attained in the 1960s and early 1970s. The history of government and the relatively new field of organizational development
present ample evidence that people are more likely to accept
decisions, gain a sense of ownership, and support actions if

they are involved in the process through which decisions are formulated and action is determined.

Students should be involved in institutional governance, but that involvement, like that of faculty, should be clearly defined and understood. Students are experts in certain areas. They are in the best position to determine if instructors communicate information and ideas in a meaningful way and get students to think creatively and critically. Students are in the best position to determine whether certain student services provide them with satisfaction and meet their needs.

A most significant question concerns at what level of institutional governance should students be involved and in what areas of college and university operations should they have a voice. Further questions relate to how students should be selected and rewarded for involvement and how they can best establish lines of communication with the students they represent.

The *Joint Statement on Rights and Freedoms of Students*, which was endorsed by most major institutional, administrative, faculty, and student national associations several years ago, stated with respect to student participation in institutional governance:

> As constituents of the academic community, students should be free, individually and collectively, to express their views on institutional policy and on matters of general interest to the student body. The student body should have clearly defined means to participate in the formulation and application of institutional policy affecting academic and student affairs. The role of student government and both its general and specific responsibilities should be made explicit, and actions of the student government within the areas of its jurisdiction should be reviewed only through orderly and prescribed procedures.[15]

Student involvement in governance at the board of control level was a matter of concern in the middle and late 1960s and early 1970s. Student leaders believed it was at that policy-making

level that they could have the greatest impact, but it may very
well be that the most meaningful student contributions can be
made at the departmental level, for it is at that point of activity
that standards and the curriculum can be developed and face-to-
face working relationships with the faculty are possible.

After an extensive study of the issues at the University of
California-Berkeley, the Select Committee on Education of the
Academic Senate expressed the belief that students could make
valuable recommendations concerning both the improvement
of courses and the development and evaluation of total academic
programs. The Select Committee contended that students brought
"a fresh viewpoint" and after exposure to the entire curriculum
were in a better position than the people who taught the courses
to point out weaknesses, omissions, and repetitive material.
Student reactions could provide a basis for knowing what had
actually been communicated as opposed to what professors
intended to teach. The mutual interests in subject matter which
students shared at the departmental level should be capitalized
upon through the organization of faculty-student committees.[16]

Summary

Administrators in colleges and universities are like managers
in business, industry, and government to a large extent. They
are responsible for stating and explaining organizational goals
and the plans attempted to implement these goals. They coordinate human resources and material assets in an organizational
structure designed to accomplish these objectives. In this process, they must plan, organize, coordinate, communicate, control,
and evaluate. Their attitudes toward, and beliefs concerning,
human motivation and behavior in work situations are important
in the establishment of trust and utilization of worker talents
and aspirations. In most areas of management in colleges and
universities, an approach valuing human beings, recognizing their
individual talents, and involving them in the decision-making
process provides the best results. However, in working with
faculty some special understandings are necessary. These understandings relate to traditions in higher education, a recognition
of the special interests of faculty members as they pertain to

rewards in higher education and the specialized nature of approaches to knowledge, and a general acceptance of the sociopolitical climate of the academic environment.

Furthermore, administrators in colleges and universities must be aware of the importance of student involvement in the development of policies and procedures that affect that student. The philosophical premise for this involvement as it improves the environment for learning can be extended to all persons who work in the college or university setting. People who are affected by decisions ought to be involved in the process through which these decisions are made. They have a reasonable idea as to how decisions will influence their behavior and they have opinions as to the best courses of action to take. Furthermore, if they are involved in the process, they will feel that they are valued and important to the entire enterprise.

Whether special interests of persons working in the academic setting are represented through advisory committees or through collective bargaining associations, they must be recognized so that compromise, synthesis, and balance are considered. Checks and balances on various perspectives are essential in the internal governance of institutions of higher education just as they are in terms of external governance. However, it must be recognized that college and university presidents, even though some may tend to assume quasi-messianic roles in which they know everything, are still in the best positions to make decisions for their institutions. Under the current legal corporate status of colleges and universities in this country, presidents are responsible to their boards of control for *all* that takes place at their institutions. They can employ faculty committees and even faculty-student-staff-alumni committees to investigate issues, evaluate programs, and make recommendations. However, the presidents cannot shift their legal responsibility to these committees, and these committees can not be held responsible for their actions in the manner that presidents are. Presidents' heads rather than the heads of committee members are always on the chopping block. This is a fact of American higher education today and any scheme, agreement, contract, or negotiation for the involvement of faculty or any other internal constituency in the governance of higher education must recognize it.

Notes

1. E. G. Bogue and Robert L. Saunders, *The Educational Manager: Artist and Practitioner* (Worthington, Ohio: Charles A. Jones, 1976), pp. 1-6.

2. Frederick W. Taylor, *The Principles of Scientific Management* (New York: W. W. Norton, 1947), pp. 9-10, 35-37.

3. Bogue and Saunders, *The Educational Manager: Artist and Practitioner*, p. 22.

4. Rensis Likert, *New Patterns of Management* (New York: McGraw-Hill, 1961), pp. 237-248; Douglas MacGregor, *The Human Side of the Enterprise* (New York: McGraw-Hill, 1960), pp. 47-57; Abraham Maslow, *Eupsychian Management* (Homewood, Illinois: Richard Irwin and Dorsey Press, 1965), p. 15.

5. H. H. Gerth and C. Wright Mills, *From Max Weber: Essays in Sociology* (New York: Oxford University Press, 1946), pp. 196-204; Herbert H. Stroup, *Bureaucracy in Higher Education* (New York: Free Press, 1966), pp. 7, 19-23.

6. Michael D. Cohen and James G. March, *Leadership and Ambiguity* (New York: McGraw-Hill, 1974), pp. 3, 121, 208-209.

7. Robert M. MacIver, *Community* (London: Macmillan, 1936), pp. 22-24.

8. Edward Gross and Paul V. Grambsch, *Changes in University Organization, 1964-1971* (New York: McGraw-Hill, 1974), pp. 173-177.

9. John J. Corson, *The Governance of Colleges and Universities: Modernizing Structure and Processes*, rev. ed. (New York: McGraw-Hill, 1975), pp. 83-85; John J. Corson, *Governance of Colleges and Universities* (New York: McGraw-Hill, 1960), pp. 27-28.

10. Corwin P. King, "Point of View: The Sad State of Faculty Governance," *Chronicle of Higher Education*, November 19, 1977, p. 48.

11. J. Victor Baldridge, *Power and Conflict in the University* (New York: John Wiley and Sons, 1971), pp. 9-11.

12. Corson, *Governance of Colleges and Universities*, 1960, pp. 98-99.

13. Corson, *The Governance of Colleges and Universities: Modernizing Structure and Processes*, rev. ed., 1975, p. 252.

14. Allan Tucker, *Chairing the Academic Department: Leadership Among Peers* (Washington, D. C.: American Council on Education, 1981), pp. 2-10.

15. William T. O'Hara and James G. Hill, Jr., *The Student/The College/The Law* (New York: Teachers College Press, 1972), p. 213.

16. University of California, Berkeley Academic Senate, *Education at Berkeley: Report of the Select Committee on Education* (Berkeley, California: University of California, 1966), pp. 60-62.

4

FUNDING OF HIGHER EDUCATION IN THE UNITED STATES

Important aspects of funding of higher education are seen through an examination of the role of the federal government, state government support, private sector involvement, and higher education and basic economics.

The Role of the Federal Government

Federal involvement has been the result of court interpretation of "to promote the general welfare" in the Constitution to include development of highways, public health, and education, and Congress has made vast grants in aid to the states for these purposes. Other than the operation of service academies and more recently some colleges in the District of Columbia, the federal government has not been directly involved in providing higher education.

The government's role in higher education has been affected significantly by armed conflict. Apparently the Civil War caused the provision that colleges offer programs in military science (Reserve Officer Training Corps, or R.O.T.C.) in order to gain land grants through the Morrill Act of 1862. Later, during World War I, students being educated in vital fields gained deferments from military service. Wars have also influenced the direction of research on college campuses.

Land grants for education started in 1787; they were continued under the Ohio Enabling Act of 1802, and whole townships of land were made available for the support of higher education. A total of thirty-one states, including California,

Oklahoma, and Oregon, received grants of this nature, but
allotments were even greater in size than townships.¹ It should
be noted that until the Morrill Act of 1862, the government
made no attempts to determine what types of educational
programs should be offered, because of the desire of the people
not to have the federal government interfere in those areas of
responsibility left to the states by the Constitution. From 1862
to this day conditions have been attached to federal grants in
the form of provisions for specific programs, and constant
battles have been waged by educational leaders to restrict the
role of the government.

The Morrill Act of 1862 mandated instruction in agriculture
and the mechanic arts, as well as R.O.T.C. programs as has
been mentioned, and it seems to have introduced the concept
of matching grants as an incentive for states to gain additional
funds from other than federal government sources. Under the
provisions of the Morrill Act, state or other nonfederal funds
had to be used for the construction of college buildings. Contract research was stated with the Hatch Act of 1887, which
provided monies for research in agriculture. The Smith-Lever
Act of 1914 established university extension services, and the
1917 Smith-Hughes Act related to vocational education. The
Morrill Act of 1890 seems to have provided a weak but initial
base for civil rights, and it prescribed more controls than the
first Morrill Act. The 1890 act specified that states could not
deny education to persons on the basis of race. At that time,
this meant that "separate but equal" facilities were acceptable.
Standards necessary for programs to maintain annual grants
under the act were presented.²

Federal assistance programs seemed to favor public institutions
because most grants were given directly to the states or to public colleges and universities through the state governments. In
wartime federal assistance went to private institutions with
military training programs, but not until 1930 was any peacetime federal assistance given to private institutions of higher
education, and these funds were in the form of financial aid
for students. The first such program was through the National
Youth Administration (1935-1943), and it amounted to an
expenditure of approximately $93 million. It has been followed

by such programs as those authorized under the G.I. Bill of
Rights of 1944, the Korean Bill of Rights of 1952, the National
Defense Education Act of 1958, aid for Vietnam veterans, and
more recent legislation, which provides for Basic Opportunity
Grants, Supplemental Opportunity Grants, College Work-Study
funds, and many other programs of both generalized and specialized natures.[3]

Legislation in 1950 authorized "the Housing and Home Finance
Agency to make up to $300 million in long-term loans to colleges,
private as well as public, for the erection of dormitories."[4] This
concept was expanded under the provisions of the U. S. Housing
Act of 1959, an act for community development,[5] and federal
support for facilities and programs has greatly increased through
such legislation as the Higher Education Facilities Act of 1963
(libraries and classrooms), the Higher Education Act of 1965,
the Education Professions Development Act of 1967, and the
Education Amendments of 1972 of the Higher Education Act.
Since the advent of contract research with the Hatch Act of
1887, expenditures for this area have been increased extensively
over the years. For example in 1950, $150 million was awarded
to a number of colleges and universities for contract research
undertaken through agreements with a dozen or so federal
agencies.[6]

Thirty years later, Johns Hopkins University was receiving
$239,869,000 from the federal government for research and
development and a total of $260,977,000 for programs and
projects that qualified for federal dollar support. Other institutions receiving substantial federal assistance in 1980 for
research and development and other projects supported by
the federal government were: Howard University, $166,146,000;
Massachusetts Institute of Technology, $163,206,000; Uni-
versity of Washington, $131,261,000; Stanford University,
$122,223,000; UCLA, $118,908,000; University of Minnesota,
$115,750,000; University of Wisconsin-Madison, $109,988,000;
Harvard University, $109,038,000; and University of California
at San Diego, $103,043,000.[7]

Another perspective on federal expenditures for higher education can be gained through consideration of total appropriations for basic research. The budget for fiscal year 1982 as

approved by the United States Congress called for a total of
$5,320,000,000 with $1,939,600,000 going to projects sponsored
by the Health and Human Services Department, $903,800,000
to the National Science Foundation, $644,800,000 to the Energy
Department, $556,600,000 to the National Aeronautics and
Space Administration, $334,200,000 to the Agricultural Depart-
ment, $77,000,000 to the Interior Department, $49,700,000
to the Smithsonian Institution, $35,700,000 to the Commerce
Department, $61,700,000 for other nondefense-agency pro-
jects, and $698,900,000 to the Department of Defense.[8]
The types of educational and related activities that are funded
by the United States government can be determined from a
consideration of the categories in the budget proposed by the
administration for fiscal year 1983. While this proposal represents
substantial reductions in many areas compared to former years and
the elimination of some categories, it does indicate areas in which
support typically has been provided. In the area of aid for students,
requests were made for the following: Pell Grants (Basic Educational
Opportunity Grants), $1,400,000,000; College Work-Study,
$397,500,000; Guaranteed Student Loans, $2,484,631,000;
National Student-Aid Commission, $345,000; veterans' education
and training, $1,665,800,000; and social security college student
benefits, $1,109,000,000. Previous budget requests included
Supplemental Opportunity Grants, National Direct Student Loans,
state student incentive grants, graduate/professional opportunities,
public service fellowships, and legal training.[9]

   In scientific research the proposal asked support for: (1)
National Science Foundation (research, program administration,
and science and engineering education), $1,077,668,000; (2)
National Institutes of Health (cancer, heart, lung and blood,
dental, arthritical, neurological, gerontological, infectious
diseases, etc.), $3,748,771,000; (3) alcohol, drug abuse, and
mental health administration, $310,248,000; (4) Department
of Agriculture, $453,293,000; (5) Department of Commerce,
$1,877,187,000; (6) Department of Defense, $828,100,000;
(7) Department of Energy, $606,070,000; (8) Environmental
Protection Agency, $108,704,000; (9) Department of Interior,
$66,600,000; and (10) National Aeronautics and Space Admin-
istration, $191,000,000.[10]

Arts and humanities funding was asked for National Endowment for the Humanities, $96,000,000; National Endowment for the Arts, $10,875,000; Corporation for Public Broadcasting, $137,000,000; and National Historical Publications and Records Commission, $286,000.[11]

For health services, funding was requested for: health resources administration (health teaching facilities, financial distress grants, aid to disadvantaged students, nursing programs, public health and health administration training, primary care/family medicine training, preventive medicine training, curriculum projects, and area health education centers), $110,200,000; and health services administration (National Health Service Corps and National Health Service Corps scholarships), $114,480,000.[12]

In the areas of educational research and statistics, civil rights, aid for minority students, institutional aid, vocational and adult education, and assistance for the physically handicapped, the administration requested financial support for: (1) National Institute for Education, National Center for Education Statistics, and for the Fund for the Improvement of Postsecondary Education, $74,292,000;[13] (2) Office of Civil Rights, Commission on Civil Rights, Equal Employment Opportunity Commission, and Office of Federal Contract Compliance Programs, $243,176,000; (3) aid to disadvantaged, migrant student college aid, developing institutions, minority institutions science improvement, and General Daniel James Memorial at Tuskegee Institute, $224,138,000;[14] (4) institutional aid (international education, construction loan subsidies, and college housing loans), $37,139,000;[15] (5) vocational and adult education (state block grants), $500,000,000; and (6) National Institute of Handicapped Research, handicapped innovation and development, personnel development, and vocational postsecondary programs, $64,491,000.[16]

In addition, the administration's 1983 budget proposal asked for funding for: bilingual training grants, $25,500,000; Peace Corps, $97,500,000; and VISTA, $231,000.[17]

Discussion of the role of the federal government in higher education requires consideration of the lobbying function because of the importance of this area for funding and legislation. Since a substantial amount of federal funding goes for

student financial assistance, consideration of lobbying in that
area should serve as a substantial example of needed efforts.
Dallas Martin, Executive Director of the National Association
of Student Financial Aid Administrators, is thought to be one
of the most successful lobbyists in Washington. According to
Thomas Wolanin, Chief Counsel for the House of Representatives
Subcommittee on Postsecondary Education, Martin is "by far
the single most effective and influential educational lobbyist
in this town." Apparently, this success is the result of the
ability to convince senators and representatives and other
influential persons that aid to students is a worthwhile investment. Martin seems to be a persuasive and logical communicator
who is highly knowledgeable and has information and relevant
facts at his command. He has had experience as a financial aid
officer and in other administrative and staff positions with a
community college, a state university, and the American College
Testing Program. This experience seems to have contributed
to his effectiveness, not only as a person who played a major
role in the passage of the Education Amendments of 1980,
but also as a principal writer of the bill's provisions.

Knowledge, persistence, experience, reason, continuous contacts with people in the field, an extensive amount of energy,
understanding of human beings in general, and ability to comprehend the political structure seem to have contributed to
Martin's success. These are characteristics all higher education
lobbyists will need, if their sponsors are to gain benefit from
the role of the federal government in higher education.[18]

State Government Support of Higher Education

These lobbying characteristics should also contribute to
positive results from contacts with state officials and legislators.
As higher educational lobbyists in Washington compete with
lobbyists who represent many other interests, state-level lobbyists
for colleges and universities find themselves in similar situations.
Many interest groups compete for state tax dollars, and the
amount that higher education receives depends upon the priority attached to higher education in comparison with public
welfare operations, health care and hospitals, environment and

recreation, highway construction and maintenance, correctional institutions, common schools (elementary and secondary schools), and vocational and technical education. Further competition for state colleges and universities comes from the private sector. Private colleges are pressuring officials and legislators to increase tuition at public institutions to create more of an open-market competition. Private colleges have also backed programs in which students use state financial aid to attend private colleges and universities. The private sector of higher education has been encouraged, since the Nixon administration policy of giving federal aid directly to students rather than institutions, to pursue this "free-market" approach. This development seems to have been responsible for some state officials taking the position that students should pay the full costs of their education.[19]

State tax dollar support for public higher education has been affected by certain economic developments. In 1972 the Brookings Institution reported that in "past peacetime years, economic growth always generated a sufficient increase in tax revenues to cover increasing government costs; but this is not the case now." Higher education is no longer a growth industry as the college market declines with decreasing birth rates. Greater interest has been emerging in nontraditional education (business schools, proprietary institutions, and industrial schools) as part of a desire to gain training in immediately applicable skills.[20]

Lyman Glenny has indicated that the number of people enrolled in these newer vocational and avocational programs is now greater than the number of persons in colleges and universities, and he believes this difference is increasing. He also emphasizes that training and educational functions now provided by such publicly assisted institutions as technical and community colleges will be taken over increasingly by businesses and industries themselves. The high cost of turnover of personnel will mean that it is more economical to provide on-the-site programs for improving skills and staff development. This will tend to further reduce enrollments at public institutions.[21]

All of these developments have a bearing on the college market, and state legislators are certainly going to be reluctant to vote

increased appropriations for what appears to be a declining
enterprise. Just as these developments relate to economic conditions, the sources of tax revenue are subject to fluctuations
in the economy. An examination of these sources makes this
clear. M. M. Chambers claims that major sources of revenue
for education at the state level are: sales taxes, income taxes,
licensing of motor vehicles and drivers, severance taxes, succession taxes, and lotteries. Sales taxes can be general and selective,
examples of the latter being taxes on motor fuel, tobacco, and
alcohol. Income taxes are either of a personal or corporate
nature with a graduated income tax tending to balance the
regressiveness of sales taxes. Louisiana uses severance taxes on
the extraction of minerals, gas, oil, and other natural resources
as its largest single source of revenue. Oklahoma and Texas also
use this type of taxation, but have other large sources of revenue.
Succession taxes cover such areas as inheritances. Property taxes
are not used for state functions, and capital improvements are
financed in a number of ways including tax dollars, bond issues,
and loans.[22]

It is not difficult to see how the business economy in a state
can influence the amount of money gained from these tax
sources. The ability of state officials to collect amounts actually
due under tax structures is another factor. In 1977 the Southern
Regional Education Board reported that a number of states
were falling short of their revenue-producing capacities. The
Board determined revenue-collecting potential by comparing
what a state actually collected with the average collected by
all states using that particular type of levy. Using this procedure,
it was determined that fourteen southern states fell 17.5 percent short of national averages, northcentral states were 9.3
percent under national averages, and mountain states were 11.2
percent under the national average. Increases in tax collections
took place from the 1974 to the 1975 fiscal year: (1) general
sales and gross receipts taxes were up 10.6 percent, but the
unused potential taxes for this period increased 19.6 percent;
(2) general property taxes increased 7.8 percent, but an additional 7.4 percent could have been realized if the potential had
been attained; (3) individual income taxes increased 10.1 percent, while the unused potential was up 16.9 percent; (4)
corporate income taxes for this period went up 10.4 percent,

but the unused potential increased 14.2 percent; (5) motor
fuel taxes increased 0.6 percent while the unused potential
was up 3.2 percent; (6) motor vehicle licensing taxes decreased
18.8 percent, but the unused potential actually increased 0.1
percent; and (7) total taxes increased 7.9 percent for the period,
but the unused potential increased by 13 percent.[23]

These differences in potential and amount collected relate to
tax dollars which might have gone for the support of private
as well as public institutions. For example, in 1979 a considerable increase in state aid for college students came about because
of an expansion in aid for those students who were attending
private institutions. The National Association of State Scholarship Programs reported that state aid to college students totaled
$852.3 million for the academic year 1979-1980, while aid for
the 1978-1979 academic year was $798.2 million. This increase
reflected a $25 million jump in aid to students attending private
colleges. Support to students enrolled at public institutions
decreased.[24] In the 1980s a decrease in federal support for
students attending private institutions could require even greater
support from state funds.

While unquestionably the most extensive state support for
private higher education is through direct aid to students, there
are other ways in which states support private colleges and universities. For example, as of April 1974, public support for
private colleges and universities was authorized in thirty-nine
states. Fifteen states have direct student aid grants for those
attending private colleges, and twenty other states have programs of grants and loans for students in both public and private institutions. Twelve states have special programs for the
support of disadvantaged students and minority groups in
private colleges. Eighteen states provide direct aid to private
institutions either through grants to specific institutions or on
the basis of students enrolled or degrees granted the previous
year. In sixteen states, aid is on a contract basis for programs
that would be expensive if duplicated by the state, but whose
graduates are scarce in society. In this area, the majority of
programs have been health-related. Support for medical education in private institutions is provided in nineteen states.
This aid comes in the form of grants and loans for students and
as grants to institutions as incentives to add more students.

Financial assistance for construction of educational facilities
is furnished in eleven states through the issue of tax exempt
bonds. Alabama and Maryland provide direct state funds for
the construction of facilities on private college campuses, and
Indiana and Michigan offer state income tax credits for individual or corporate donations to private colleges. Also, Michigan
has exempted state private colleges from gasoline taxes, Virginia
exempts private colleges in the state from sales taxes, Illinois
provides funds for consortia of private colleges, New York
endows chairs for scholars at both public and private institutions,
South Carolina allows private colleges and universities to make
purchases through the state purchasing office, and Minnesota
allocates funds to private colleges participating in instructional
television and library programs.[25]

Disparate patterns are discernible in state funding of private
higher education. Perhaps even more confusing is the discrepancy among states with respect to the degrees to which they
fund higher education in their own public colleges and universities. Some states, particularly in the West, Midwest, and
South, seem to place a great deal of faith and responsibility for
higher educational needs of their constituencies in public institutions. In the East and the Northeast, a long tradition of
private institutional responsibility for higher education has
had a continuing influence. Only the massive influx of veterans
into postsecondary education in the late 1940s seems to have
broken this pattern, especially in Connecticut, Massachusetts,
New Jersey, and Pennsylvania. The land-grant influence and
tradition in agricultural states has been significant. This influence
and tradition seem to include a tenet that colleges and universities receiving tax dollar support from the people ought to be
responsive to the needs of those people. All of this involves
political beliefs and inclinations toward support of Populism,
the Grange, the Wisconsin Progressive Party, and probably
more recently, the Farm Labor Party in Minnesota. At any rate,
there are differences between the East and the West. A consideration of state government support of higher education for
1982-1983 can be perceived in three different ways. First, if
the total amount of dollars appropriated for higher education
by states is considered, the following rankings appear:

1.	California	$3,274,865,000
2.	Texas	2,035,534,000
3.	New York	2,010,001,000
4.	Illinois	1,029,282,000
5.	Florida	905,796,000
6.	Pennsylvania	870,965,000
7.	Michigan	865,000,000
8.	Ohio	846,331,000
9.	North Carolina	793,432,000
10.	Virginia	616,475,000

Using a similar "top ten" ranking, a different configuration appears when appropriation for public higher education on a *per capita basis* is considered. The following is relevant:

1.	Alaska	$356.37
2.	Wyoming	197.56
3.	Hawaii	188.70
4.	North Dakota	164.95
5.	New Mexico	138.62
6.	Texas	137.85
7.	California	135.35
8.	North Carolina	133.28
9.	Iowa	131.46
10.	Kansas	130.94

Another perspective on the situation of state support for higher education becomes evident when appropriations *per $1,000 of personal income* are considered. On this particular basis, the following rankings achieve relevance:

1.	Alaska	$25.91
2.	Hawaii	17.10
3.	Wyoming	16.94
4.	New Mexico	16.26
5.	North Dakota	16.14
6.	Mississippi	15.81
7.	Utah	15.56
8.	North Carolina	15.41
9.	South Carolina	14.69
10.	Texas	12.85

These measures of state support of higher education, taken
from "Analysis of State Funds for Higher Education" in the
Chronicle of Higher Education, October 20, 1982 concern different perspectives.[26] One concentrates on total dollars, a dimension that gives the most populous states an advantage.
Another focuses on dollars spent per person in the state. The
third perspective considers the number of dollars spent on
higher education out of $1,000 personal income for each citizen.
All of these approaches have a certain amount of legitimacy,
but one of the most poignant comments concerning state expenditures on public higher education was made by John D.
Millett, former President of Miami University and former Chancellor of the Ohio Board of Regents, when he said:

> Ohio as a state was simply not disposed to support
> its public higher education on generous terms. I
> often asked many different persons for an explana-
> tion of this situation and I never found a satisfac-
> tory answer. It appeared to me that the wealthy
> social, economic, and political leaders of the State
> sent their sons and daughters to the major private
> colleges and universities of the East. Everyone was
> well aware that men in the Taft family were Yale
> men. The state universities existed to provide edu-
> cational opportunity for the sons and daughters
> of school teachers, preachers, the artisans and
> other middle class citizens, and there was no need
> to spend any undue amount upon their education.[27]

Millett's comment encompasses a wide range of values, con-
victions, and beliefs, and it hits at the very heart of higher
education in America. While a number of leading citizens
professed a strong belief in education as a great equalizer, they
never really made a complete commitment to that belief and
opted for a type of subtle elitism in which vast private fortunes
could go toward the support of private institutions of higher
learning while the holders of those fortunes professed a strong
commitment to the kind of public education that tax dollars
supported in Ohio. A consideration of the variety of financial

support to private higher education, as opposed to the kind of backing state-assisted colleges and universities receive, seems to prove the point made so well by Millett.

Private Sector Involvement in Higher Education

It was estimated that voluntary support from individuals, corporations, foundations, and religious denominations for colleges and universities in the United States for 1979-1980 was $3.8 billion. A single gift of $105 million was made to Emory University from the Emily and Ernest Woodruff Fund. According to the Council for Financial Aid to Education, the ten leading institutions in terms of voluntary support received in 1979-1980 were (1) Emory University, $115,592,443; (2) Harvard University, $76,179,576; (3) University of California system, $74,972,959; (4) University of Texas system, $60,722,404; (5) Stanford University, $60,122,303; (6) Yale University, $59,649,269; (7) University of Pennsylvania, $49,129,330; (8) Cornell University, $47,288,245; (9) University of Southern California, $42,234,069; and (10) University of Minnesota, $40,568,067.[28]

Another perspective on private sector support of American higher education is presented through consideration of the specific sources of voluntary support. On the basis of a survey of 1,019 private and public colleges and universities, the Council for Financial Aid to Education reported that for 1979-1980 gifts came from the following sources: business corporations, $555,754,198 (18.2 percent); religious denominations, $124,248,875 (4.1 percent); alumni, $725,540,650 (23.7 percent); nonalumni individuals, $677,997,246 (22.2 percent); foundations, $739,759,188 (24.2 percent); and other sources, $231,752,435 (7.6 percent).[29]

In 1981 the Council for Financial Aid to Education presented information on thirty years of voluntary support for higher education which showed that total support was $240,000,000 in 1949-1950, $815,000,000 in 1959-1960, $1,780,000,000 in 1969-1970, and $3,800,000,000 in 1979-1980.[30] This support is more significant for private institutions than for public colleges and universities as can be seen from the following information on the sources of support for 1979-1980 operating

SOURCE OF REVENUE	PERCENT OF REVENUE	
	Private Institutions	Public Institutions
Educational and general revenue	76.1	81.7
Tuition and fees	31.9	13.9
State government	1.4	46.5
Federal government	16.6	11.3
Local government	--	3.9
Private gifts and grants	*10.2*	*2.1*
Endowment income	7.1	0.3
Other	8.9	3.7
Auxiliary enterprises	11.4	11.0
Hospitals and independent operations	12.5	7.4

expenses at private and public institutions of higher education.[31]

The actual financial status and progress of privately supported institutions during recent years have been shown through reports of W. John Minter and Howard Bowen. Their reports have covered a number of years of responses to the question: "In what ways are independent colleges and universities gaining ground, holding their own, or losing ground?" Their conclusions have also been based upon study of reports institutions prepare annually: (1) Higher Education General Information Survey (HEGIS) on enrollment, salaries, and finance; (2) salary information as submitted to the American Association of University Professors; (3) audited financial statements and supporting schedules; and (4) a voluntary support survey. Income and expenses have been analyzed as to how they relate to the Consumer Price Index and student enrollments. Included within the survey sample have been: research universities, universities granting doctoral degrees, comprehensive universities and colleges, selective liberal arts colleges, less selective liberal arts colleges, and two-year colleges.[32]

For a number of years institutions were able to hold their ground through drawing upon endowment income for operating expenses, deferring plant and equipment repair, and keeping faculty and staff salaries below inflation levels.[33] However, reports issued in 1982 showed that many public and private institutions were no longer holding their own in the economic market. Income figures adjusted for inflation revealed that revenue received had decreased 1.9 percent from 1979 to 1980 when calculated on a per student basis at public colleges. Private colleges and universities realized a 1 percent gain in this area during this period only because of increases in revenue at larger universities. Most private institutions experienced losses in income from 1979 to the 1980 fiscal year.[34]

The future does not appear favorable with respect to the financial support of higher education, especially private colleges and universities. Unless maintenance improves, depreciated facilities and equipment are replaced, reserve funds are restored, institutions stop drawing on endowment for operating expenses, and faculty and staff salaries are improved, great danger is in store for many private institutions which have provided an essential alternative to public education. These sentiments were expressed in the 1970s and must be echoed even louder in the 1980s. The situation has become even more serious when reduction in state and federal assistance to students at private colleges and universities is considered. Students at many private institutions have been receiving substantial financial assistance through state and federal aid programs. For example, Hiram College in Ohio educated approximately 1,000 students through the expenditure of $10,695,499 for fiscal year 1981. During that year Hiram students received $1,250,626.90 from state and federal government sources in the form of student aid. It is reasonable to assume that a substantial part of that money came back to the institution as tuition and fees. Total revenue from tuition and fees from 1981 was $4,840,939. Any significant change in state and federal policy on provision of financial assistance to students attending private colleges will have a

definite influence on the opportunity of many students to
attend Hiram. Students at many other private colleges would be
affected in a similar manner.[35]

Higher Education and Basic Economics

The problem of private colleges and universities can be attrib-
uted in part to economic conditions. Economic factors also
have had a significant effect on the public sector of higher education. Therefore, some consideration of higher education and
basic economics might be appropriate.

Education might be considered as an *economic good*, using
"good" in the sense of goods and services. This good is influenced by general forces in the marketplace and might be viewed
from three perspectives: as a *commodity* purchased for immediate consumption; as an *investment* from the viewpoint
of the person obtaining the education; and as a *capital good*
which benefits society in general.

Education as a good in the free market of a capitalistic system
is subject to supply and demand conditions, and these conditions relate to production and consumption. Four major elements
appear necessary in the production of an economic good or service: natural resources, capital, labor, and technology. In higher
education, natural resources might mean a number of factors.
The student to be educated might be the natural resource, which
is turned into a finished product through the process of education—an application of technology (teaching and learning processes) by a labor force (the faculty, staff, and administration
of the institution). Capital might pertain best to the buildings
and property and equipment holdings of the institution. Some
of these comparisons become rather farfetched, and it becomes
apparent that higher education differs from other phenomena
with respect to how it relates to aspects of economic systems
and the economy as a whole. Volume in most businesses and
industries means lower unit costs and larger profits (up to a
point of diminishing returns), but for higher education larger
volume promises larger deficits and possibly poorer quality.[36]

Seymour Harris has stated other differences:

Ordinarily the consumer seeks to buy in the cheap-
est market, but this is not necessarily true of the
buyer of higher education. He is often prepared to
pay the high rather than low price.

The dominant seller does not determine the
price for the service (higher education). If this were
so, tuition and fees in the West for private institutions would approximate charges for public colleges
and universities.

... higher education by its very nature is a high
labor user and its wage and salary bill has been
forced up by rising productivity and consequent
increases in real wages.[37]

Traditions related to academic prestige and quality of education are connected to lower student-to-faculty ratios, and
this makes it difficult to reduce the size of the labor force
substantially without creating some problems in the academic
setting.

Another difference between business practices and higher
educational procedures, although both business and education
function in the same general economic environment, is that
most businesses and industries seem to include their capital
costs (construction of new facilities and depreciation) in what
they charge the consumer for their goods and services. Higher
educational institutions do not.

Many colleges make no regular allowance for depreciation, amortization, or repair and maintenance of
physical plant, with the result that their costs are
higher and plant value lower than they realize, and
eventually a large repair bill catches them with no
reserve.[38]

In 1959 Harris said:

No college, unless the money is borrowed, includes
as part of its cost the capital charges. I estimate
these capital charges on the basis of a forty-year

life and four percent interest at about $400 per
student. At Harvard I estimated the capital cost per
student at roughly $1,000; yet the treasurer's report
does not so much as mention a building.[39]

In 1979 Hans Jenny criticized college and university fund
accounting and the complicated financial statements this accounting approach produces. A number of his arguments were
along lines similar to those that Harris presented twenty years
earlier. Jenny commented on depreciation costs not being
shown in current expenditures. He observed that a plant re-
placement component is not built into the process, and this
cost element has been mushrooming.[40]

Viewing higher education from the perspective of what it
does for the individual and what it might accomplish with respect to that individual's attitudes toward society, a statement
from William Ammentorp is relevant:

The contribution of education to quality of life is
entirely an individual matter and can lead to decisions to purchase education which cannot be de-
fended in a cold analysis of the market potential of
the training received.[41]

While the influence of education on the quality of life of an
individual is difficult to measure, efforts have been made to
measure the impacts of colleges and universities on the economics of their communities. In Baltimore it was reported that
during the fiscal year 1980 Johns Hopkins University and its
hospital spent $326 million directly or indirectly, including
payment of $7.8 million in city property taxes by employees
of those institutions and by the institutions themselves. Services
provided by the city for the institutions' students, staff, and
faculty and their dependents amounted to only $30 million,
a figure that included public schooling and the $527,154 cost
to the city of tax exemptions received by the University and
the hospital. The Association of Independent Colleges and
Universities in Massachusetts reported for the 1981 fiscal year
that private higher education was responsible for raising total

personal income in the state by $3.6 billion, saving $242 million
in tax dollars that would have been needed had students in
private colleges been educated at state expense, and increasing
employment by 177,000. The presence of St. Louis University
was reported to have had an economic impact of $252 million
on its metropolitan community, Harvard personnel and operations added almost $106 million to Cambridge in 1979-1980,
Missouri private college and university students and employees
spent $352 million in 1979, and the 106 colleges of the New
York Commission on Independent Colleges and Universities
were estimated to have had a total economic impact of almost
$8 billion on the state in 1978.[42]

Attempts to apply quantitative measures to the value of an
education to an individual in terms of earning power have also
been made. However, arguments for increased earnings as a
result of advanced educational attainment are becoming weaker.
In 1974 the United States Census Bureau estimated that a male
with a college degree could expect to earn $758,000 in a lifetime
while a male who finished high school could expect to earn
$479,000. In 1972 the average yearly income for a man with a
college degree was $16,200; for a man who was a high school
graduate, the average yearly income was $10,430.[43] In 1980
Lee Ellis was among people who were raising questions about
higher education as an investment:

> Over the last few decades, calculations have been
> made of the rate of return on the "college invest-
> ment" when these costs and losses in income are
> taken into account. The 1940-60 rate of return
> held at roughly 12 to 15 percent—which is pretty
> hard to beat. However, Freeman and Holloman
> placed the 1969 rate at 11 to 12 percent and the
> 1974 figure at 7 or 8 percent. So now the balance
> has shifted: The stock market will generally yield
> an average return of at least 10 percent over the
> long haul, and, if you want something with no
> risk, certificates of deposit at a bank guarantee at
> least 7½ percent, plus a free alarm clock in your
> choice of four decorator colors.[44]

Maybe it is time to recognize that quality of life for the individual just cannot be measured in numerical terms. Educators
in their zeal for quantification and spirit of overempiricism
have forgotten that the most important dimensions of the
college experience are above and beyond any mere dollars and
cents price tags.

Summary

While the United States Constitution provided that education
would be the responsibility of the governments of the states,
higher education has not been without federal involvement.
The promotion of general welfare has furnished the rationale
for such involvement, and military conflict and national defense have been the primary stimulants for federal spending
on higher education with the exception of the monumental
land-grant acts, which furnished impetus for the education of
students in agriculture and the mechanic arts. Substantial support for students in more recent years has come about because
of a general philosophy beginning in the 1950s that resources
should be available for the student whose individual and parental
finances are insufficient to cover higher education expenses. A
major departure from that approach has come through the policy
of a 1980 Republican administration which has sought to reduce
substantially the federal government role in higher education
with the exception of research related to national defense.

This reduction in spending will influence state government
support, which has varied from state to state but pertains to
both public and private institutions. In the case of the latter,
support has been principally through student financial assistance although states have aided private colleges and universities
in other ways. As state and federal support for private higher
education may be decreased because of economic conditions
and new federal policy, an additional burden will fall on the
private sector. Support from private individuals, corporations,
and foundations has been substantial over the years, but dollars
for support have not kept pace with inflation. Colleges have
had to sacrifice to survive. Deferring maintenance, not replacing
equipment, not restoring reserve funds, and keeping faculty

salaries at levels not matching inflation mean that dangerous conditions are ahead for both public and private institutions.

Developments concerning the funding of higher education hinge on the question of its value to society as well as to the individuals who receive degrees. Efforts have been made to show the economic impact of educational institutions on their communities, but it is essential to recognize that the major contributions education makes to life, vitality, and the downright survival of a society cannot be measured.

Notes

1. John S. Brubacher and Willis Rudy, *Higher Education in Transition: A History of American Colleges and Universities, 1636-1976*, 3d. ed. rev. and enl. (New York: Harper and Row, 1976), p. 227.

2. Ibid., pp. 227-229.

3. Ibid., pp. 230-231.

4. Ibid., p. 232.

5. Harold C. Riker with Frank G. Lopez, *College Students Live Here* (New York: Educational Facilities Laboratories, 1961), p. 114.

6. Brubacher and Rudy, *Higher Education in Transition*, p. 231.

7. "Fact-File: U. S. Funds for Colleges and Universities—The Top 100 Institutions in Total Federal Obligations for Fiscal 1980," *Chronicle of Higher Education*, March 31, 1982, p. 10.

8. "Fact-File: Federal Appropriations for Basic Research for Fiscal 1982 Compared With Fiscal 1981," *Chronicle of Higher Education*, January 20, 1982, p. 15.

9. "Student Aid," *Chronicle of Higher Education*, February 17, 1982, p. 17.

10. "Scientific Research," *Chronicle of Higher Education*, February 17, 1982, p. 19.

11. "Arts and Humanities," *Chronicle of Higher Education*, February 17, 1982, p. 20.

12. "Health Manpower," *Chronicle of Higher Education*, February 17, 1982, p. 21.

13. "Education Research and Statistics," *Chronicle of Higher Education*, February 17, 1982, p. 21.

14. "Civil Rights," *Chronicle of Higher Education*, February 17, 1982, p. 22; "Minorities, Disadvantaged Students," *Chronicle of Higher Education*, February 17, 1982, p. 22.

15. "Institutional Aid," *Chronicle of Higher Education*, February 17, 1982, p. 23.

16. "Vocational, Adult Education," *Chronicle of Higher Education,* February 17, 1982, p. 23; "Handicapped," *Chronicle of Higher Education,* February 17, 1982, p. 23.

17. "Miscellaneous," *Chronicle of Higher Education,* February 17, 1982, p. 23.

18. Anne C. Roark, "Washington's Most Effective Lobbyist for Higher Education," *Chronicle of Higher Education,* October 6, 1980, pp. 3-4.

19. Lyman A. Glenny, "The 60s in Reverse," *Research Reporter* 8, no. 3 (1973): 1-3.

20. Ibid., p. 3.

21. Lyman A. Glenny, "Demographic and Related Issues for Higher Education in the 1980's," *Journal of Higher Education* 51 (July/August 1980): 377.

22. Merritt M. Chambers, *Higher Education: Who Pays? Who Gains?* (Danville, Illinois: Interstate Printers and Publishers, 1968), pp. 200-201.

23. "Tax Collections: Rates in Most States are Below U. S. Average," *Chronicle of Higher Education,* April 25, 1977, p. 7.

24. "States Adding $25 Million to Aid Private College Students," *Chronicle of Higher Education,* November 5, 1979, p. 13.

25. Jack Margarrell, "39 States Using Variety of Approaches to Aid Private Colleges," *Chronicle of Higher Education,* April 1, 1974, p. 7.

26. "Fact-File: Analysis of State Funds for Higher Education," *Chronicle of Higher Education,* October 20, 1982, p. 9.

27. John D. Millett, *Politics and Higher Education* (University, Alabama: University of Alabama Press, 1975), pp. 15-16.

28. Jack Magarrell, "Corporation's Gifts to Colleges Up 25 Pct. in 1980; Smaller Increase Likely This Year," *Chronicle of Higher Education,* May 18, 1981, pp. 1, 9.

29. "Fact-File: Voluntary Support for Colleges and Universities in 1979-80," *Chronicle of Higher Education,* May 18, 1981, p. 8.

30. "Fact-File: 30 Years of Giving to Higher Education," *Chronicle of Higher Education,* May 18, 1981, p. 8.

31. "Chronicle Survey: Sources of College and University Revenue in Fiscal 1980," *Chronicle of Higher Education,* January 13, 1982, p. 12.

32. W. John Minter and Howard R. Bowen, *Independent Higher Education Fourth Annual Report on Financial and Educational Trends in the Independent Sector of American Higher Education* (Washington, D. C.: National Association of Independent Colleges and Universities, 1978), pp. 3, 109.

33. Jack Magarrell, "Hidden Decay Seen Afflicting Private Colleges," *Chronicle of Higher Education,* July 28, 1980, p. 1.

34. "Higher Education's Hard Times Have Begun, Survey Shows," *Chronicle of Higher Education,* January 27, 1982, p. 4.

35. Hiram College, *1980-81 President's Report* (Hiram, Ohio: Hiram College, 1981), pp. 5-6.

36. Philip H. Coombs, "An Economist's Overview," in *Financing Higher Education, 1960-70*, ed. Dexter M. Keezer (New York: McGraw-Hill, 1959), pp. 12-34.

37. Seymour E. Harris, "Financing Higher Education: Broad Issues," in *Financing Higher Education, 1960-70*, ed. Dexter M. Keezer (New York: McGraw-Hill, 1959), p. 53.

38. Coombs, "An Economist's Overview," p. 23.

39. Harris, "Financing Higher Education: Broad Issues," p. 53.

40. Hans Jenny, Address to the Department of Educational Administration Doctoral Residency Seminar at Kent State University, Kent, Ohio, October 30, 1979.

41. William Ammentorp, "The Finance of Higher Education," mimeographed (Minneapolis: University of Minnesota, 1977), p. 14.

42. Jack Magarrell, "More Colleges Marshal Data to Demonstrate Their Economic Impact," *Chronicle of Higher Education*, March 10, 1982, p. 8.

43. "Males Earn $758,000 With College Degree," *Chronicle of Higher Education*, April 8, 1974, p. 6.

44. Lee Ellis, "A Dollar-and-Sense Look at the Value of Education," *Midwest Quarterly* 21 (Winter 1980): 223-224.

5

BUSINESS AND FINANCIAL OPERATIONS

Higher education's survival in times of scarce dollars and high costs of energy, supplies, and services depends to a large extent on the insight, efficiency, and resourcefulness of the chief business officer. In addition, this administrator is in a key position to influence all activities of the institution. He or she has access to information, an understanding of the implications of this information, and influence over, if not direct control of, functions of the institution that probably dictate the course of all other operations. The position of the chief business officer, therefore, is an appropriate point of departure for discussion of business and financial areas in higher education. Examination of the responsibilities of this officer involves an overview of accounting, budgeting, and financial reporting; trends influencing business operations and results of these trends; problems caused by these trends; and some possible solutions.

Responsibilities of the Chief Business Officer

A 1974 publication of the National Association of College and University Business Officers presented the responsibilities and duties of the chief business officer through the specification of four comprehensive categories: administrative management, business management, fiscal management, and financial accounting and reporting. Within the general classification of administrative management, institutional planning and design and operation of management information systems are relevant. This area also includes fiscal administration and sponsored

programs (where agencies and organizations outside the college
or university provide funds and prescribe goals for research and
services), management of risk reduction and insurance programs,
legal services, management of student aid funds, and administration of personnel programs, faculty and staff benefits, labor
relations, and collective bargaining.

Business management duties include purchasing, auxiliary
enterprises, physical plant operation, maintenance, planning,
construction, and security and safety programs. Fiscal management responsibilities concern the administration of endowment
and similar funds (money given with the stipulation that the
principal will not be spent but interest will be used for support
of a specified service or program), management of investments
(funds invested to produce income for the institution), budget
preparation and budgetary accounting, internal control and
audit, and institutional research and resource management.
Financial accounting and reporting encompass the development
and maintenance of the basic accounting and records system
of the institution and the preparation of financial reports and
analyses.[1]

With respect to the human resources of colleges and universities,
the chief business officer has overall responsibility for the administration of the program that recruits, assigns, pays, evaluates,
promotes, and terminates secretaries, clerks, custodians, maintenance workers, and all other nonteaching personnel of the
institution. In public institutions, these are usually people
who are part of a classified service system of employment and
frequently members of a state employees' union. People who
serve as staff members or administrators on an annual contract
basis in the areas of student services, academic affairs, public
information, institutional advancement, fund raising, community
relations, and alumni affairs are usually not included among
these personnel.

Chief business officers have major responsibility for those
services or enterprises that are directly or indirectly related to
the educational activities of the institution. These services are
provided for students, faculty, and staff and in the main are
expected to generate sufficient income to pay for their operation. They usually include dormitories or residence halls, food

services, bookstores, student unions or student centers, intercollegiate athletics, and similar educationally related endeavors.
These services are in general financed through a charge to their
users or a specific fee charged to all students. The services are
classified as auxiliary enterprises for management and accounting
and reporting purposes.

Historically, the first auxiliary enterprise in American higher
education was probably the dormitory housing provided for the
young men attending colonial colleges. It grew from the medieval Oxford and Cambridge traditions when rural settings of
those institutions made housing accommodations necessary. It
related to the colonists' desire for a quasi-cloistered environment,
which could provide for the religious development of students.
Since American colleges in the eighteenth and nineteenth centuries were in rural localities, housing was essential. A tradition
evolved that dormitory living was an important part of educational development. Students were thought to grow intellectually
and socially through living and studying together. In many cases
this remained the ideal rather than becoming an actuality as
far as intellectual development was concerned. Student emphasis
was on the social aspect of this situation.

The *in loco parentis* concept, which dominated institutional-
student relationships for many years, was also influential in the
development and maintenance of auxiliary services. It was believed that young people needed to be placed in a situation in
which control, guidance, and discipline could be exercised in
a similar manner to parental discipline provided in the home.
Through the years, it has been maintained that college conditions and expectations differ vastly from those in secondary
schools, so a "bridge" is needed to provide for the students'
transition from one environment to another. In the case of
dormitories, the objective has been to see that students studied
and met academic standards.[2]

Justification for other auxiliary services such as student health
programs, recreation, and intercollegiate athletics has appeared
to be on the same basis; these services or enterprises help to
maintain students in a state of physical, social, and psychological
fitness that enables them to gain the most that they possibly
can from classroom learning. This bridge and support concept,

even with changes from the *in loco parentis* idea, still seems to be at the base of services for the "traditional" student, and it can be extended to relate to the needs of the "nontraditional" learner who has returned to formal education after raising a family or pursuing a career that technology has now made obsolete. For these students, the bridge that auxiliary services can provide may extend to institutional maintenance of day-care centers, tutorial service, and counseling and information sessions furnishing the opportunity to discuss common concerns and apprehension about the return to formal education. Day-care centers, tutorial services, and counseling and information may go beyond a strict definition of auxiliary services; they might be supported with money received from student fees and tax dollar subsidies rather than being self-supporting; and they might be under the direction of the chief student affairs administrator. However, the chief business officer, through responsibility for the budget and financial controls, can influence these areas. Auxiliary services and related counseling and advising activities, because of their influence upon human development in the long run and student morale in the short-range perspective, constitute important aspects of overall educational endeavors. Chief business officers also influence other areas, the importance of which may be less conspicuous but is nevertheless significant for institutional climate. Campus security provides a good example of one of these areas. Campus security on college and university campuses is, for the most part, a responsibility of the chief business officer, although this area may come under the jurisdiction of a director or vice president for administrative services, if the institution has such a position. Because of the open nature of many state or community institutions and their desire to serve as many political, social economic, recreational, and cultural interests as possible, all elements of the general public have access to these institutions. Members of the public become involved in college and university life from illegal as well as legitimate perspectives. College and university security and law enforcement officers need to have the training, experience, and leadership to deal with the problems this situation presents. How they treat potential and real offenders and their victims has significant implications for feelings of well-being, security, and justice in the academic community, and the chief business officer usually provides the administrative leadership for this area and is accountable and responsible for its successes and failures.

Accounting, Budgeting, and Financial Reporting

While the influential position of the chief business officer in the areas of auxiliary enterprises and campus security might be of a subtle nature as far as impacts on the institution are concerned, the domains of accounting, budgeting, and financial reporting might indicate a more direct influence. Nevertheless, financial and business affairs of colleges and universities can be considered from the perspective of the classifications concerning the manner in which revenue is received, the way it is allocated for human and material resources, and the way these financial transactions are reported. This consideration not only provides another dimension for viewing the business and financial affairs area, but adds further support to the argument that the chief business officer is in a most crucial position in American higher education.

The purposes of clear accounting and reporting procedures for colleges and universities are similar to those for private business and industry. These goals are to: (1) facilitate effective and efficient management of the procedures through which revenue is received and resources are used; and (2) provide information to the public, creditors, and investors so that management effectiveness in meeting organizational goals can be determined. The profit motive for private business and industry seems to mean the difference. In commercial business, the money that is realized through the business is supposed not only to replenish the resources used in business operations but also to show a profit for investors. In higher education, the aim is to offer programs and services that meet society's needs and interests. Profit is not expected.[3]

There are also differences between higher education and business that are brought out through accounting procedures. Specifically, colleges and universities use fund accounting, accrual accounting, accounting for investments, and depreciation. Institutions with religious affiliations also follow some different accounting and reporting procedures because of those connections. Financial statements for colleges and universities differ from those used in business and industry in format as well as content.

Businesses and industries make money from the sale of products. Only a portion of the revenue needed to provide programs and services at colleges and universities is received from tuition and fees charged to students. Income is received from many other sources, and there is a need to account to sources of funding to indicate that funds are being used correctly and effectively. This "stewardship" accounting to sources of funding has resulted in the implementation and maintenance of fund accounting. It means that a most important purpose of any system of accounting and financial reporting is to communicate to people who provide money for colleges and universities that their money is being spent wisely and efficiently for the purpose they have specified. The evolution of a system that meets these requirements has produced a whole set of classifications, reports, and a uniform language unique to higher education.

Procedures for fund accounting are influenced by the purposes, restrictions, and rules specified by the sources of funding for the use of these funds and by governing boards of colleges and universities. Whether purposes, restrictions, and rules are the responsibility of governing boards or have been established by outside agencies is extremely important in terms of accounting and reporting. Each fund, and there are usually six major classifications of funds or fund groups used by higher educational institutions, is a relatively self-contained unit "with a set of self-balancing accounts consisting of assets liabilities, and a fund balance."[4]

The six fund groups are: Current Funds, Loan Funds, Endowment and Similar Funds, Annuity and Life Income Funds, Plant Funds, and Agency Funds.

Current Funds are the expendable resources an institution uses to support instruction, research, and public service activities. In other words, these funds cover operating costs for a given period of time. Two major classifications of expenditures exist within Current Funds groups: educational and general expenditures

and auxiliary enterprises costs. The latter category seems to be
the result of the principle that auxiliary services should generate
sufficient income through some charge to users of these services
to pay for the cost of providing these services. The National
Association of College and University Business Officers suggests
that the following functional classifications be used with the
Current Funds group in budgeting, accounting, and reporting
in the area of educational and general expenditures:

>   Instruction
>   Research
>   Public Service
>   Academic Support
>   Student Services
>   Institutional Support
>   Operation and Maintenance of Plant
>   Scholarships and Fellowships

The category of instruction covers the expense of academic
departments and includes expenditures related to salaries for
professors and instructors, graduate assistants, student clerical
assistance, and secretaries and clerk-typists in the academic
departments. It also covers any staff benefits paid to teachers
and full-time secretaries and what might be paid for any supplies, telephone, postage, and travel expenses incurred or to
be incurred. If any new equipment is to be purchased, it is
included within this category. Similar expenses for research
and public service projects are covered under designations in
those two general categories. Expenses for academic deans'
offices and the library are included in the academic support
category, and the area of student services encompasses any
expense related to admissions, records and registration, financial aid administration, counseling, career planning and job
placement, new student orientation, student activities, and
student health. The classification of institutional support
provides a category for expenses in the areas of the president's
office, the business office, parking, traffic and security, alumni
relations, fund raising, news services and public information,
management information and data processing, and other opera-

tions that affect the entire institution. Operation and maintenance of physical plant expenditures cover the costs of human and material resources and energy necessary to maintain buildings for instruction and support services. The category of scholarships and fellowships includes all expenses related to scholarships and fellowships over which the institution has the authority to decide on recipients. Money in the Current Funds group can be transferred to other funds groups either on a mandatory or nonmandatory basis.[5]

Loan Funds are those monies that can be used by faculty, staff, and students with the provision that repayment will be made. A number of avenues are open for disposition of repayments. A loan fund can be distributed on a revolving basis, in which principal and interest payments are made available to new borrowers, or provisions can specify that repayments are to return to the person originally making the grant or gift used for the loan. Gifts and grants with these stipulations are augmented in Loan Funds by income from the investment of endowment monies whose earnings can be used only for loans; grants from the federal government that are refundable when institutions agree to use their own monies to match these grants; interest payments on loans; and investments of Loan Funds. Money from the Loan Funds group can also come from transfers of Current Funds group monies that are controlled by the college or university and are transferred for the purpose of matching refundable grants from the federal government, and from unrestricted money in the Current Funds group area that the institution's board of trustees wishes to be used for loans.[6]

Endowment Funds that colleges and universities use are of three types. The first type is the basic endowment fund, which is a sum of money given to the institution by an individual donor or some agency outside the institution. This money is given with the stipulation that the principal is not to be expended but invested, and the interest it produces is to be considered as present and future income for the institution. The institution may either spend this income or add it to the principal. The second type of endowment is called Term Endowment. It is like basic endowment with the exception that the institution is allowed to use a part or all of the principal after a designated

period of time has elapsed or when a certain event has taken
place. The third type of fund in this category is a Quasi-endow-
ment Fund, and it involves money the governing board, instead
of some person or agency outside the institution, has designated
as endowment to be retained and invested.[7]

Annuity Funds are related to property and money that come
under the control of a college or university because the donor
requires that the institution agree to pay him or her, or another
party designated by the donor, stipulated sums of money at
specified times. A termination time for payments is specified
in the agreement. This area is discussed in further detail in the
chapter on institutional advancement.[8]

Life Income Funds are similar to annuity funds. Institutions
gain the use of money or property with the stipulation that
they pay the donors or other designated parties an income on
a periodic basis. This income is derived from the assets donated
and usually covers the lifetime of the income beneficiaries.[9]

Agency Funds are those that an institution holds as custodian
or fiscal agent for either individual faculty members, staff
members, or students, or for organizations of faculty, staff, or
students. When the amounts of money in these funds are small,
one combined fund report of assets and liabilities of the Current
Funds group is sufficient. Separate fund groups are not necessary
under those circumstances.[10]

In addition to the fund categories already discussed, an institution may be responsible for other funds which are to some
extent similar to the Endowment and Agency Funds groups.
Pension funds are representative of these funds. They are treated
through procedures very much like those applied to Endowment
and Agency Funds groups.[11]

Plant Funds encompass unexpended monies that purchase
land, construct buildings, or relate to gaining other "long-lived"
assets serving college or university objectives. This subdivision
of the Plant Funds group is referred to as Unexpended Plant
Funds. The general category of Plant Funds includes money
designated for replacing and refurbishing buildings and other
property, a subgroup called Funds for Renewals and Replace-
ments. The general classification of Plant Funds also covers
funds going toward payment of charges for debt service and

debt retirement on money borrowed to construct buildings, a subgroup specified as Funds for the Retirement of Indebtedness. The Plant Funds group also provides for an accounting of the cost, or value at the time given, of "long-lived assets" that are not endowments.[12] It indicates the base for the funding of these assets and shows any liabilities connected to this source. This final subgroup is referred to as Investment in Plant and it includes costs actually incurred in land purchases, improvements, buildings, movable equipment, furniture, library books and film strips, and construction in progress.[13] The source of assets for the four subgroups are (1) agencies outside the college or university; (2) fees and assessments coming directly from students through an obligation incurred by the institution's board to take care of debt service or other physical plant commitments (this agreement specifies that the board has no right to use these funds for any other purpose); (3) transfers, either required or not required of the board, from other funds groups; (4) borrowing from agencies outside the college or university; (5) borrowing from other funds groups within the institution; and (6) earnings from investments of funds in subgroups.[14]

Certain procedures, practices, and rules govern interfund transferring, and usually three types of statements are used to report this and other financial activity of colleges and universities. These statements are (1) a balance sheet, reporting as of a particular date, "a series of fund groups, with each having its own self-balancing assets, liabilities, and fund balances"; (2) a statement of changes in fund balances, indicating activity affecting fund balances of groups during the fiscal year or other period being reported; and (3) a statement of current fund revenues, expenditures, and other changes. The balance sheet is roughly comparable to a checkbook because it shows assets minus liabilities or credits minus debits and the resultant balance for each of the following: Current Funds, Loan Funds, Endowment and Similar Funds, Annuity and Life Income Funds, Plant Funds, and Agency Funds. The statement of changes in fund balances indicates revenues and other additions, expenditures and other deductions, mandatory and nonmandatory transfers among funds, other additions and deductions such as prior year encumbrances, net increase or decrease in the fund

balance, and the actual fund balance for the end of the fiscal
year. The statement of current fund revenues, expenditures,
and other changes furnishes detailed information concerning
the current funds part of the statement of changes in fund
balances. It indicates the source of revenue and the way the
money was actually spent during the fiscal year.[15]

Supplementary schedules and materials and notes to financial
statements are used to provide additional information, but
these three statements provide a "big picture" of overall operations of the college or university.

The many accounts related to these statements are maintained
through what is termed accrual accounting. When money is
earned, it is reported, and when goods or services are received,
they are presented as expenses. Depreciation is not reported as
an expense nor is any expense involved in acquiring capital
assets for the college or university. On the date for closing a
balance sheet for an operation, expenses incurred by the closing
date are "accrued" and expenditures applicable to future periods are considered "deferred" expenses. A situation in this
kind of accounting involves not reporting some deferrals and
accruals related to interest on student loans and investment
earnings. The rationale for this nonreporting is that these transactions do not have significant influence on the financial statements. However, financial statements can be affected by orders
to purchase goods or services even though these goods and
services have not been received or delivered by the end of the
period for the financial statement. They are not balance sheet
liabilities nor are they expenditures to be reported on a statement of current fund revenues, expenditures, and other changes.
These purchase commitments are considered to be "encumbrances" and are "charged" against the relevant fund balance in
this way because they do have a bearing on the financial picture
of an operation at a given time.

Since the property, buildings, and equipment holdings of
colleges and universities are considerable, attention must be
given to depreciation of these assets because it affects the
economic value of institutions. However, the nonprofit status
of colleges and universities seems to make a difference in financial reporting here as opposed to that for private businesses and
industries. Depreciation in physical plant assets is not reported

in the current funds part of the statement of changes in current fund balances nor is it designated in the statement of current fund revenues, expenditures, and other changes. The rationale for this practice is that higher educational financial reporting is supposed to show only resources gained and expended rather than being an expression of net income. This practice is subject to debate because it confuses the "true" picture of a "business." Nevertheless, "capital asset acquisitions financed from current funds *are* reported as expenditures of that group in the year of acquisition."[16]

> That depreciation is not recorded in the current fund does not preclude the use of expired capital cost data in evaluating performance and making management decisions on a variety of operating activities. Also, for purposes of statement presentation, depreciation allowance may be reported in the balance sheet and the provision for depreciation reported in the statement of changes in the balance of the Investment in Plant subgroups of the Plant Funds group.[17]

With respect to the Endowment and Similar Funds group, it is acceptable in college and university financial circles to indicate depreciation on investments which are held as depreciable assets, so that principal and income can be kept separate. When investments are considered, their purchase is reported at cost, but if investments are received as gifts, they are reported at fair market or appraised value when they are actually received. An allowable option is to report investments at fair or current market value, if this reporting basis is standard for *all* investments in all funds. College and university financial reporting and accounting procedures are complicated further when religious group property and services are factors in institutional operations.

The whole point in this discussion of higher educational accounting and financial reporting is that special understandings are necessary. Most of the intricacies of this area are fathomable only to accounting and business management specialists; yet, principles, procedures, and practices, in this area influence all programs and services of the institution. How they are inter-

preted and understood by faculty, staff, students, trustees, and
other institutional "publics" depends upon the values, integrity,
intelligence, and ability to interpret and communicate of the
chief business officer.

Trends Influencing Business Operations and Results of These Trends

General economic trends, featured by constantly rising prices
without a drop in these prices since World War II, have hurt
higher education because revenues have not kept up with increasing costs. In January 1980 it was reported:

> Goods and services for which a typical college or
> university paid $1,000 in 1970 cost $1,794 in 1979.
> If costs increase no faster than the 6.7 percent rate
> of the 1970s, the same goods and services in 1989
> would cost $3,444.[18]

Enrollment predictions for 1988 as compared to 1979 are
that part-time students will increase 3.7 percent but full-time
students will decrease 9.3 percent. Since the number of students
enrolled is the major basis for state subsidies and fees paid, this
prediction has important implications. The enrollment of full-
time students has most import, since the amount of subsidy
legislators provide and the tuition students pay for full-time
study is sufficiently more extensive than that for part-time
students.[19]

Another general influence on the financial operations of
institutions of American higher education is the crisis in energy
sources. It was reported in September 1977 that during the
fiscal year of 1976-1977 the prices paid for utilities increased
17.8 percent. Other comparisons showed that utilities costs
increased 8 percent for 1975-1976, 28 percent for 1974-1975,
and 23 percent for 1973-1974.[20]

The results of these trends appear to have produced greater
accountability because of the increased competition for limited
tax dollars and the dollars students have available to spend for
their educations. Dollars just do not appear to go as far as they

once did in terms of supporting, or paying for, higher education. Lags in the economy of states that depend rather heavily upon sales taxes have also caused a limit on the number of dollars that are earmarked for the support of education. It would seem that when dollars are scarce, taxpayers want to know that maximum benefit is gained from any expenditure of their tax dollars. Legislators feel this pressure, and the economic priorities of their electorates become crucial. If the attainment of technical skills means that more people can obtain employment, the "sensitive" legislator is most likely to support technical-vocational programs as opposed to more advanced education in the postsecondary realm.

When dollars are scarce and their buying power is diminished, greater central control at the state level seems to emerge as a foremost priority. Uniformity in terms of procedures for the allocation of funds seems to become important. Further stress is placed upon the development of management information systems to provide relevant data for decision making. Planning, programming budget systems become important because they seem to provide some type of objective, rather than "subjective" and political, criteria for the allocation of funds to educational endeavors. This "objective" approach is accompanied by a further emphasis on the evaluation of programs and managerial performance concerning those persons who are assigned responsibility for the success of programs.

The development of formulas or program models for the allocation of funds emerges from the economic development in which financial resources for higher education become limited. The idea is that certain types of programs, whether they are to be offered at the state's prestigious "flagship" university or at an emerging state teachers' college-state university, still cost the same. For example, a freshman English course at Ohio State University should essentially cost the same amount of dollars as a similar course offered at Youngstown State University. The models for this approach theoretically take into consideration that different disciplines (English, physics, sociology, and physical education, for example) require different expenditures and these expenditures vary further according to the level at which instruction is being given. The rationale is that a doctoral program in physics will certainly cost more than a freshman-level course in political science.

Economic developments also seem to produce an awareness that strategic planning is important. Planning is discussed in Chapter 9.

Problems Caused by These Trends

Because of the emphasis on greater accountability to the general public, state officials attempt to become more involved in college and university policies and practices. This has been discussed in Chapter 2. However, it seems appropriate to cite a specific example of this involvement in business and financial operations. In 1976 State Auditor Thomas E. Ferguson criticized Ohio University for maintaining a separate student center for blacks when its main student center was losing money, operating a university press at a loss, and leasing university facilities at low rent to a research firm owned by a professor from the University.[21]

This situation shows that persons who have a particular control over the purse strings seem to believe that they also have the authority to become involved in educational philosophy and objectives. The matter of a black student center at Ohio University involves an understanding of several centuries of racism and efforts to correct that condition. Final decisions in this area transcend the special interest financial perspective of a state auditor and should involve persons who have both a cognitive and affective appreciation for the problems from philosophical, legal, sociological, and economic perspectives. The views of a state auditor should receive attention, but they are not the dominating factors for policy and practices in this situation. Also, the maintenance of a university press, regardless of what it costs the institution, may be a prime factor in that university's justification for existence as a scholarly and research-oriented institution.

There are dimensions of an academic institution that are hard to measure in an auditor's ledger. These dimensions relate to broad goals and responsibilities and a commitment to improve the human condition in every way possible, if higher education is to realize its fullest potential.

An additional problem is the lack of understanding and communication between and among board of trustees members, administrators, legislators, students, and faculty. The jargon of formula budgeting, systems approaches, and simulations and models for strategic planning has blocked communication because nobody wants to appear ignorant, ask questions, and admit confusion. Harold Howe, II, Ford Foundation Vice President and former United States Commissioner of Education, cites the following as a source of communication problems between political leaders and persons supposedly responsible for American higher education: "The tendency of practitioners of policy science to develop their own mystique and the parallel tendency of politicians to act as if they understood it."[22]

What is inferred in Howe's statement is that board of trustees members and legislators have been dazzled by footwork and jargon of the so-called experts in policy studies and social sciences, a group that is not too unlikely to include college and university presidents.

Howe's comments are relevant with respect to another problem. Along with the solutions of policy scientists, management techniques such as planning, programming budget systems and other "textbook" approaches have been viewed as panaceas for financial problems in higher education. Howe believes that these techniques have been oversold and states their shortcomings:

> The most significant of these limitations is in the elusive area of values. Men do things or they don't, in part because of their beliefs in what is right or wrong, important or unimportant, in their interest or contrary to it.
> Neither the formulation of positions that are defined by value judgments nor their sorting out through politics, whether in the faculty meeting at the university or the state legislature or the United States Congress lend themselves to ultimate resolution by social science analysis.[23]

Howe expresses the belief that the ultimate decisions for programs and priorities rest with the institutional president and his or her value judgments regardless of the sophisticated techniques employed to present and analyze data.

In this connection, special concern should be directed toward increased reliance upon computers, data processing, and management information systems. If administrators in policy and decision-making positions do not gain more knowledge of computers, they may lose their positions of authority and influence to the computer experts, who tend to approach education from a technological special interest point of view.

Another consideration in this area is that college administrators need to understand at what point they have sufficient data and the necessary knowledge of it to make decisions. All the data available will not be important unless decision makers know how to weigh information and determine which data are really significant for particular policy directions and decisions.

Significant problems arise when there is an overreliance on formulas in the allocation process for funding state colleges and universities. The dependence upon formulas may mean neglect of studying specific needs, problems, and expectations of separate institutions. Lee Beck has stated:

> Despite a quarter of a century of development since
> the California faculty staff procedure was conceived,
> formula budgeting has failed to prove its utility.
> Formulas have failed to recognize and embrace the
> full diversity of higher education in the functions
> or functional priorities of the institutions; in levels
> of instruction or methods of teaching; in innovation;
> or in quality.[24]

Juanita Kreps, former Secretary of Commerce and former Vice President of Duke University, provides further rationale for questioning the advantages of formula budgeting and the application of productivity measures to higher education. She has pointed out the difficulty in determining the monetary value of the final "product" of a college or university education. Using constant formulas for calculating the cost of educating a student does not take into account the changing "product" of higher education over the years. Kreps has argued:

> As long as we continue to treat our output—the
> certified student—as the same, regardless of any
> changes in his quality as measured by his projected
> contribution in dollar terms, educational productiv-
> ity will appear to be declining because we seem to
> be producing the same good at higher and higher
> costs.
>
> If educational productivity is redefined as a measure
> of costs relative to returns, educators will be freed
> from the relentless drive toward increasing the
> number of students we teach, and charged instead
> with the responsibility of improving educational
> quality.[25]

Ever-increasing bureaucratic structures in which procedures
become more important than services and results can constitute another problem for the financial welfare of institutions
of higher education. When institutional bureaucracy alienates
people through its impersonalization, these people and those
to whom they relate their experiences can become indifferent
if not hostile concerning the financial needs of that college or
university.

A further problem concerns adversary relationships which
appear to become more acute as financial support declines.
When the need arises for programs and people to be cut, whether
these reductions are to be made in the public or the private
sector, self-interests and survival of people become the crucial
determinants. In such situations, faculty can become particularly
interested in collective bargaining and staff members recognize
the importance of classified service system protection and state
employee unions. Protection of self-interests also seems to mean
more reliance on the courts and the law for an interpretation
of relationships and problem solutions. All of this can mean
that institutions can fall into rigid patterns of relationships,
which make them less receptive to student and societal needs.

Some Possible Solutions

With these complications in human relationships and the
implications these situations have for financial and business

operations, consideration of possible solutions attains a high
level of importance. Colleges and universities should give
major attention to openness and attempts to communicate in
a clear and concise way with all constituencies. Gene Budig,
Chancellor of the University of Kansas in the 1980s, has stated
that college presidents should take advantage of every opportunity
to explain programs and services and their finances to students,
faculty, staff, and legislators. They should welcome the chance
to answer questions from these persons and to speak of the
strength and contributions of their colleges and universities.[26]
He believes:

> Historically and tragically, state legislators have
> found college and university representatives hard
> to communicate with and difficult to comprehend.
> Too often their questions about the academy and
> its programs have drawn abstract answers that have
> left them more perplexed than before. There has
> been without a doubt a breakdown in communica-
> tion.[27]

Budig believes that university officials, when informing legislators of institutional programs and financial needs, should be
"Armed with a mass of technical budgetary data which they
can translate into understandable terms, terms that legislators
will comprehend and appreciate."[28]

These officials must emphasize that institutional programs
and services meet the needs of the people who vote and that
it is good politics to support these activities.

Another important step to take in attempts at solving financial
problems is to involve people in the process through which
financial policies are formulated and decisions are made. People
who represent higher educational interests should attempt to
educate decision makers and policy makers in terms of the
strengths and shortcomings of the technology, data processing,
computer programming, and the use of these tools in the determination of educational programs and plans. Initially college
and university presidents need to gain comprehensive understandings in these areas. This can help them to educate board
members, influential citizens, and legislators.

Efforts to evaluate programs and their products in a realistic manner must be continued in the ongoing task of showing taxpayers and donors that dollars spent on higher education do promote the welfare and interests of society in a variety of ways.

The principal agents for communication in these areas are chief business officers. However, while they are in the best position to communicate with corporate leaders, heads of philanthropic organizations, and legislators, they are only as strong and authentic as the programs and services their institutions provide. All of the practical knowledge and acumen of the chief business officer cannot compensate for programs and services that are irrelevant to the needs of the persons who are expected to finance them.

Summary

The chief business and financial officer of a college or university occupies an important position in higher education. It may very well be the most significant role in higher education in terms of influencing financial support from local, state, federal, and private sector sources. Board members who have ultimate responsibility for institutions are essentially persons with backgrounds in business and industry. Effective communication with these persons and legislators requires an understanding of economics and finances. The individual with the best knowledge in these areas at colleges and universities is the chief business officer. Furthermore, that chief business officer usually comprehends computer language and mentality because his or her area is the most likely in the collegiate setting to use management information systems and apply computer technology. Because of the fiscal accountability nature of transactions with the federal government, the chief business officer is in the best position to fathom all of the intricacies of such involvement. Regardless of the political beliefs an individual holds concerning the role of higher education in the United States of America, the best evidence indicates that the business world and corporate power are the major determinants for policies, practices, procedures, and, above all, funding at American colleges and universities. What person other than the chief business officer is in the best position to understand and interact with these influences, providing that institutional programs and services are what they are advertised to be?

Recognition of the significance of the role of the chief business and financial officer at American colleges and universities may be the only honest salvation of higher education, providing that this officer maintains his or her integrity, recognizes humanism, and admits that there are undeniable shortcomings in efforts to measure and quantify the human condition.

Notes

1. National Association of College and University Business Officers, *College and University Business Administration* (Washington, D. C.: National Association of College and University Business Officers, 1974), p. 7.

2. John D. Millett, *Planning, Programming, Budgeting for Ohio's Public Institutions of Higher Education* (Columbus, Ohio: Ohio Board of Regents, 1970), pp. 96-98.

3. National Association of College and University Business Officers, *College and University Business Administration*, pp. 177-178.

4. Ibid., p. 178.

5. Ibid., p. 187.

6. Ibid., p. 191.

7. Ibid., p. 192.

8. Ibid., p. 194.

9. Ibid., p. 195.

10. Ibid.

11. Ibid., p. 196.

12. Ibid., p. 197.

13. Kent State University, *Financial Report, June 30, 1981* (Kent, Ohio: Kent State University, 1981), p. 4.

14. National Association of College and University Business Officers, *College and University Business Administration*, p. 197.

15. Ibid., p. 178.

16. Ibid., p. 179.

17. Ibid.

18. Jack Magarrell, "The 1980's: Higher Education's 'Not-Me' Decade," *Chronicle of Higher Education*, January 7, 1980, p. 6.

19. Ibid., p. 7.

20. "Higher Education's Index of Inflation Goes Up 6.4 Pct.," *Chronicle of Higher Education*, September 6, 1977, p. 13.

21. *Cleveland Plain Dealer*, August 4, 1976.

22. "Ford Aide Warns Colleges on Management Panaceas," *Chronicle of Higher Education*, May 13, 1974, p. 5.

23. Ibid.

24. Leland E. Beck, "The Advantages and Disadvantages of Formula Budgeting for State Supported Colleges and Universities," (M. A. thesis, Kent State University, 1975), pp. 122-123.

25. "High Quality Seen Lifting Education's Productivity," *Chronicle of Higher Education*, May 13, 1974, p. 5.

26. Gene A. Budig, *Academia and the Statehouse* (Lincoln, Nebraska: University of Nebraska Press, 1970), p. 37.

27. Ibid., p. 19.

28. Ibid., p. 20.

6

INSTITUTIONAL ADVANCEMENT

There are some important aspects of the lives of colleges and universities that are influenced more by emotion and sentimentality than by logic and rational processes. When an alumnus or alumna speaks of his or her alma mater, it is frequently with nostalgia and thoughts and feelings of better times. The philanthropist who has contributed to many worthy causes has a special warmness toward the college library he built, and everybody in the state of Nebraska feels extra proud when the Cornhuskers win in the Orange Bowl. Notre Dame has been said to have the largest collection of loyal boosters among cab drivers and persons from every walk of life and religious persuasion of any institution of higher learning in the country. These "subway alumni" constitute a vital force in the perpetuation of the reputation of the University of Notre Dame as a leading center of higher education, just as much as its faculty and graduates do.

Any comprehensive attempt to understand American higher education requires that this emotional dimension receive attention. As has been discussed in the consideration of special influences on higher education, people in positions of responsibility and power make both major and minor decisions on the basis of their beliefs, personal experiences, and "gut-level" feelings, regardless of the acceptable, rational, and analytical justifications they might offer after the fact to support their actions. While such emotions and beliefs are more easily hidden in the realms of academic programs, business and financial policies, and interinstitutional cooperation and competition, they really become blatant when intercollegiate athletics, alumni relations, and fund-raising activities are taken into consideration. It is difficult for college administrators and trustees to hide behind logical and reasonable approaches when the commitment of funds and energy to these areas is examined.

In a rather subtle manner, colleges and universities seem to recognize the significance of emotion and individual perceptions in the organizational patterns that have emerged in American higher education. Further, these emerging patterns indicate an awareness of the personalized or subjective impact of human experience on communication. At least, the evolving system of governance takes into account that institutions are perceived differently among the many groups, if not individuals, who have a stake in their welfare. This claim is made because responsibility for communication and public information is frequently included among the duties of the administrative officer who supervises activities in the areas of alumni relations, fund raising, and in some cases, intercollegiate athletics. This officer may be a vice president or director charged with the task of coordinating and leading in institutional advancement, college or university relations, public affairs, external relations, or development. However, regardless of specific title, he or she is the specialist in human emotion and what it can mean for a college or university.

Communication and Public Information

While no one administrative officer can assume responsibility for the clarification of communication and dissemination of information among the many groups of people, internal and external, who have an interest in the institution, the person in charge of public affairs or university/college relations must be especially sensitive to certain realities in this area and attempt to accommodate them. Organization is *communication*. Common understandings of symbols, terms, concepts, and ideas keep people moving in the same direction toward the accomplishment of specific as well as general goals. A college or university functions on the basis of the common understandings its personnel hold in terms of its long-term as well as day-to-day objectives. If the various groups that constitute the institution do not understand each other's objectives, functions, and special interests, effort can be wasted, antagonisms can arise, and progress toward the accomplishments of tasks and goals is impeded. An atmosphere where anxiety and suspicion prevail can replace one of trust, mutual understanding, and general well-being. Because of differences in background, education, and interests, individuals and groups within and outside the university or college have different views of events and issues.

The individual responsible for internal communications needs to make every effort to insure that there is an exchange of ideas and views among students, faculty, administrators, and clerical and support services staff. The student press, institutional information bulletins, the campus radio station, and all other internal media should be used to facilitate this exchange.

Specific communication responsibilities of the vice president or director of college or university relations, or whatever the title, include the world external to the institution. Duties include contact with the media, news releases, and other such forms of information for the public. How events on the campus, particularly those of a negative nature, are presented and interpreted has a significant bearing on the attitudes of the public toward the institution. Millard Roberts, the controversial Presbyterian minister who in the early 1960s built Parsons College of Fairfield, Iowa, from an institution of 250 to one with an enrollment of over 3,000, is credited with saying that any publicity, good or bad, should be welcomed because it makes people aware of the institution. He was supposed to have made this statement when *Life* magazine featured Parsons College, emphasizing such institutional practices as allowing students to attend classes regardless of grades as long as they continued to pay tuition.

Other college leaders have taken a position somewhat different from that of Roberts. They have said that publicity or public information should promote educational goals. This is with the acknowledgment that some information going out to the public, while not advancing those objectives, helps to keep the institution in the public's mind. News releases on student accomplishments, reports of campus events, visiting lecturers, concerts, and faculty achievements are in this category. The news media may not be especially interested in such releases and reports, particularly

when options are coverage of more sensational misdeeds of
student pranksters and scandals involving mismanagement or
misappropriation of funds and fraudulent practices in awarding
grades and degrees. Negative publicity of this nature is inevitable
in the public's mind. News releases on student accomplishments,
attempt to hide it. Questions must be answered openly and
honestly except where confidentiality and privacy are issues.
In such cases, administrators may have to maintain silence.[1]

Ronald W. Roskens, president of the University of Nebraska,
accentuated the need for openness and honesty with the public.
When Vice President at Kent State University, he stated that the
public should be made aware that larger state universities represent society in microcosm and that negative as well as positive
events take place on campus, just as they do in society in general.
This reality cannot be disguised because of its potentially un-
favorable influences on legislators, citizens, and many other
"publics" who in some way or other provide support for the
institution.

One of the first writers to use the expression "publics" for
those groups with whom it is important for administrators to
be honest was Clarence A. Schoenfeld. Writing in 1954, he said
that there were five significant publics with whom university
administrators should be concerned: "the student, the professor,
the trustee, the public at large, and the 'university family' groups."
Areas of emphasis thought to be important to these publics were
teaching, student welfare, research, public service, community
relations, parental rapport, alumni loyalty, employee esprit,
and professional acceptance. He also referred to the significance
of what he called "the big picture" and "housekeeping." The
former was defined as "the gamut of fundamental spiritual
characteristics of the campus culture," and the latter as "the
range of managerial functions." He matched his publics with
areas of emphasis and decided that teaching and student welfare were crucial for the student; research and the "big picture"
were foremost concerns for the professor; the public at large
should have public service; parental rapport, alumni loyalty,
and employee esprit were essential for university family groups;
housekeeping was major for the trustee along with professional
acceptance and community relations.[2]

Schoenfeld believed that an institutional president could use
these key perspectives as a public relations checklist because
he considered good public relations to be "inextricably linked
with sound administration in all its aspects."[3] While Schoenfeld
expressed these ideas almost thirty years ago and there may be
many other publics in the 1980s who are actively involved in
the affairs of colleges and universities, his point is well taken
that balanced management, which attempts to take into account
as many important perspectives as possible, can promote positive
attitudes toward the institution. In the language of public
relations, it can lead to a good image.

The keen competition for students in the declining market
of the 1980s has caused many colleges and universities to take
a more assertive approach in presenting a positive image to their
publics. Emphasis has been on marketing institutions to attract students, although certain marketing practices have been
characteristic of some institutions for many years. The University
of Michigan solicited students for its law program through
newspaper advertisements run in Chicago, Cincinnati, Detroit,
New York City, St. Louis, and Washington, D. C., in 1859.[4]
In recent years public relations and marketing consulting firms
have been retained to assist in such projects as market analyses,
production of radio and television commercial announcements,
newspaper and magazine advertisements, and the writing of
brochures. While these may be important measures for presenting
and explaining the programs and services of the institution,
they can in no way substitute for concrete and effective educational endeavors that actually meet the needs of publics and
accomplish their expressed objectives. They can not substitute
for a dedicated, capable, and concerned administration, faculty,
and staff who genuinely believe in serving people. While the
public service role of institutions of higher education will be
discussed in Chapter 8, it is necessary at this point to give
attention to an important aspect of that role. The best public
relations people, and they would probably be insulted by being
so labeled, for land-grant institutions such as the University of
Wisconsin, University of Minnesota, Michigan State University,
University of Nebraska, University of Tennessee, and University
of Georgia, are those cooperative extension workers who relate

to people in all corners of their states in an effort to solve community problems through a citizen-expert-grass-roots partnership. Part of the rationale for the substantial tax dollar support that state universities have received over the years in most Midwestern agricultural states has been the recognition that these institutions have provided worthwhile services to citizens, which have not only increased their incomes but have improved the total quality of their lives.

Historically, the farmer whose dairy herd had been saved from an epidemic of mastitis through the diagnosis and quick action of an extension specialist from the university had very strong emotional feelings about the value of that institution. No public relations firm could ever create that favorable an image. The United States may no longer be an agrarian-oriented society as it was when the land-grant colleges were thriving, but the formula for success in public relations is still the same. It is still production of positive results that counts.

Intercollegiate Athletics and Public Information

While the Midwest has been known for its prowess in the area of agricultural production, it has also gained recognition for its collegiate athletic teams, especially for the football teams in the Big Eight Conference. Intercollegiate athletics, sometimes included within the general organization area with the functions of public information, communiations, fund raising, alumni relations, and other external relations programs, constitute an important factor in the operations of many colleges and universities. There are some realities in intercollegiate athletics that appear to deserve attention.

Acknowledging that abuses in major college sports are legion, there are some overriding influences and conditions that mean that intercollegiate athletics are, and will continue to be for some time, forces to be reckoned with in American higher education. Many persons with athletic talent, blacks in particular,[5] have been incredibly exploited. High school transcripts have been altered, and normal admissions procedures have been bypassed for outstanding high school football players. There are even cases in which academic deficiencies have been made up through an athlete's enrollment in a nonexistent course.[6]

The policies and practices of some of the leading academic institutions in the United States have been questionable as far as providing equal opportunities for women in the intercollegiate athletic realm. Many arguments have been raised by colleges and universities to prevent affirmative action, which appears so necessary to overcome years of institutionalized sexism in college sports, and when women's programs are given any genuine encouragement, these efforts seem to result in those programs moving down the same path of exploitation and commercialism that have been followed for years in men's programs. Attempts have been made to approach the issue of affirmative action in college sports in a logical manner. George LaNoue has asserted that the evaluation of intercollegiate athletics should be on the basis of two dimensions: participant value and spectator value. He has recognized that women gain something of value, and can be involved in, major revenue-producing men's programs. In spite of the obvious sexist overtones, examples might be that cheerleaders and homecoming queens seem to derive benefits from the "big" football game.[7] A seventy-seven-year-old grandmother's letter to her son may be more appropriate to illustrate that it isn't just participants that appreciate and benefit from intercollegiate athletics:

> Brr—winter is really here with 12 to 18 degree temperatures at night. Friday we had our first snow. The football field was swept clean and the snow removed from the seats. After all these years, Dad and I know how to bundle up for cold weather so that we keep warm.
>
> What do you think? Your old mother finally made TV! During the game, a young man from Channel Three stopped and interviewed a few people in the crowd. He asked if I would answer some questions— I said "sure." He wanted to know why we come out for games on a cold day for a losing team. I told him we were loyal Badger fans and had been coming to every game since 1938.[8]

Even though people other than direct participants seem to gain from intercollegiate athletics, major college sports have been attacked for being "big business." In 1976 it was reported that the National Collegiate Athletic Association (NCAA) had seven hundred institutional members, a staff of forty-three, a headquarters in a $1.5 million building, and an annual public relations budget of $250,000. In that same year, the NCAA held a two-year television contract with the American Broadcasting Corporation for $16 million, each major football bowl participant received $175,000 plus $30 per mile one-way for travel expenses, the NCAA had a $4 million dollar contract for television coverage of its basketball tournament, and the NCAA had a 297-page manual of rules for the practices and procedures of its members. At least 10 percent of the Association's members had violated at least one regulation in the manual.[9]

Faculty members have been appalled by practices in the area of intercollegiate athletics and constantly seem to oppose expenditures for competitive sports whether these costs involve activities at the small college or the major university level. They cite such evidence as that presented in an April 15, 1974, report of the Kent State University Chapter of the American Association of University Professors. This report referred to national research of the American College Testing Program that indicated that only 2 percent of students state that intercollegiate athletics are an important factor in their choice of college. This was consistent with local findings for Kent State University where 37 percent of students surveyed indicated that curricular programs were influential in their choice.[10]

This statistical information has been cited to combat the notion that intercollegiate sports records help attract students and give colleges and universities national exposure. On the other hand, this notion of the influence of sports is supported by such evidence as President Stephen Horn's claim that six minutes of prime time coverage of Long Beach State's program in the arts, during that institution's nationally televised appearance in the NCAA basketball semifinals, exposed more persons to the university's activities than had learned about the institution through reading newspapers since its inception in 1949.[11]

In support of intercollegiate athletic program value, the importance of intercollegiate athletics in the establishment and maintenance of cohesiveness and esprit de corps for the institutional population and the larger community in which the college or university is located has been stressed. James B. Long has stated that a value of intercollegiate athletic programs is:

> To provide a focal point for the morale, spirit, and loyalty of the students, alumni, and friends; to offer a common ground where enthusiasm is shared by all and the university may be strengthened and united.[12]

Also, with emphasis upon Title IX of the Education Amendments of 1972 and affirmative action, the spectator value of athletics has gained greater attention, largely because major athletic powers have sought rationale for maintaining revenue-producing programs in football and basketball at their current levels without providing similar participant programs for women.[13]

In addition to publicity and spectator value, backers of intercollegiate athletics cite the edge that participation in athletics gives to the competitor in the American economic system. Individual testimonials as to the benefits of intercollegiate competition for life are numerous. For example, former black athlete Melvin L. Reddick, three-year starting end at the University of Wisconsin in 1967-1969, tri-captain and United Press Honorable Mention in 1969, a two-year letterman in basketball, and now an attorney in the records section of the Law Department at the Columbia Broadcasting System in New York City, states:

> I learned that there are certain rules which govern activities in sport and life. If you learn how to play by the rules and work with others, you can be successful in whatever you choose to pursue in life.[14]

Dial Hewlett, Jr., Chief Medical Resident at Harlem Hospital Center in New York City and Clinical Fellow in Medicine at Columbia University's College of Physicians and Surgeons in 1979 (440- and 660-yard dash man and co-captain of the University of Wisconsin track team that won the Big Ten Indoor Championship in 1970), claims, "I obtained a sense of dedication and appreciation for hard work during my athletic career at the University of Wisconsin. The same attitude carried me through the rigors of medical school."[15]

Gerald L. Kulcinski, Professor of Nuclear Engineering at the University of Wisconsin and an outstanding end on 1958, 1959, and 1960 University of Wisconsin football teams, has asserted that:

> My athletic experience at Wisconsin taught me the value of teamwork when facing a complex and tough problem. Additionally having played under some of the finest coaches at Wisconsin, I was able to see how men conducted themselves under stress and still ended up with self-respect, win or lose.[16]

There is little research evidence to support the values given to participation in sport by such athletes as Mel Reddick, Dial Hewlett, and Gerry Kulcinski. With respect to the influence of participation in sport on personality development, there are insufficient research data to conclude that competition in sport builds character, molds leaders, and helps persons to persist, endure, overcome failures, and succeed in other areas of life. Robert Singer, a leading sports researcher, has refuted these claims and cited the highly personalized basis on which the benefit of sports competition is frequently judged:

> Never have so many said so much with so little research support. Personal observations and experiences permit each of us to have some insight into this aspect of sport. After all, the things that athletes and coaches do and don't do, on the field and off, are subject to extensive media coverage.

> These activities reflect on the personality, or aspects
> of the personality, of the individual. Since general-
> ized inferences tend to dominate our thought
> processes, there is little wonder that some exposure
> to, some incidents in, and some experiences with
> sport would lead to conclusive feelings about *all*
> sport.[17]

George Leonard has challenged claims made for the value of
athletic competition. He argues that an interpretation of Social
Darwinism, which glorifies survival of the fittest and praises
fierce competition in sport, was used by industrialists in later
years of the nineteenth century and early in the twentieth
century to justify cruel competition in business. Promotion of
competition in business was on the basis of the merit of natural
selection of predators. Leonard expressed the belief that this
was a distortion because Darwin himself had emphasized that for
human beings "the highest survival value lies in intelligence, a
moral sense and social cooperation, not competition."[18]

However, all of these logical challenges, even in the academic
environment where reason should prevail, seem to fall on deaf
ears. Intercollegiate athletics have been and remain important
factors in higher education. Some presidents have used athletics
to promote their institutions and have made little attempts to
hide this. An outstanding example is the case of Michigan State
University. That institution had a sound base from its establishment in 1855, and that foundation was reinforced by land-grant
legislation in 1862, but the real achievements, growth, and
status came in the 1940s, 1950s, and 1960s. The person who
led that institution in those decades was John Hannah, and it
has been said about him in the 1940s that:

> Dr. John A. Hannah, president of Michigan State
> College, as it was known then, had a dream in the
> 1940s. Under his direction, the little land-grant
> college of 7,000 was growing quickly and he
> wanted to make it one of the nation's great univer-
> sities. However, Hannah was having trouble lining
> up a large and competent enough faculty. Most

of the men he wanted had never heard of Michigan
State, although it had been in existence since 1855.
One way to gain recognition, Hannah reasoned,
was to have a good football team.[19]

President Hannah did build a major football team as well as a
major state university, and he is supposed to have said that
"if it meant the betterment of Michigan State . . . our football
team would play any eleven gorillas from Barnum and Bailey
any Saturday." [20] In more recent years, another widely acclaimed
research, land-grant university made a commitment to football,
and this commitment was made even in the dire economic straits
in which most of higher education finds itself in the 1980s. In
the winter of 1982 it was announced that Jackie Sherrill would
receive $287,000 per year (a six-year contract for a total of
$1,722,000) as athletic director and football coach at Texas
A and M University. This was believed to be the highest salary
ever paid an administrator in college sports. At that time it was
reported that Barry Switzer, head coach of football at the
University of Oklahoma, was receiving $150,000 per year in-
cluding outside income, Paul Bryant who held a similar position
at the University of Alabama was earning $115,000 annually,
and football coaches at major universities were averaging between
$45,000 and $60,000 per year. As a basis for comparing the
salaries of football coaches with those of other college administrators, a 1980-1981 survey by the College and University
Personnel Association was cited. According to this survey, only
fifty-three college and university officials earn $90,000 or more
per year. Officers included in this number were eighteen presidents
or chancellors of systems or individual institutions, thirty medical
deans and executives of health-related units, one executive
vice president, one academic vice president, one chief planning
officer, and one director of intercollegiate athletics. Football,
basketball, and other athletic coaches were not included in
this survey.[21]
    The logical conclusion in the situation of intercollegiate
athletics is that emotional involvement or appraisal is far more
significant than any rational analysis at even the more prestigious academic institutions. For the most part, any individual

who has ever really been involved in athletics judges from a very personal perspective, as Robert Singer has implied. If the individual doing the evaluating is a former athlete in any way, means, or shape, his or her heart tends to dominate assessment. This appears to be a particular consideration in American society from the perspective of both the participant and the spectator. Two examples can be cited. In the first, consideration of male machismo connected to sport provides insight. While this particular incident relates to a fictional story and professional sport, it seems to prove the point. To establish the setting for this situation, it should be said that Willie Hammer, a baseball star in Tom Wolfe's *Mauve Gloves and Madmen, Clutter and Vine*, is about to make a television commercial. A number of people who have interest in this commercial are on the sound stage. One of these people is a man with "a big nose," who is an important executive with the sponsor. Hammer describes this situation:

> With everybody standing there, my friend with the nose let me know he'd played a little ball himself, in college some place. He just slipped it in, but he made *sure* he slipped it in, if you know what I mean, and I like that too. It's a thing I've noticed everywhere, and this man, this executive of a big corporation like Fabrilex, he was no different from anybody else. This country is full of about 100 million men who played a little ball, some sport, some time, some place. And whenever it was, it was there they left whatever feeling of manhood they ever had. It grew there and it bloomed there and it died there and now they work at some job where the manhood thing doesn't matter and the years roll by. But they've got this little jar of ashes they carry around . . . I once played a little ball . . . . They see a professional athlete, and it stirs up the memories. . . . They can feel the breeze.[22]

In the second case, the significance of athletics is in the nostalgic value it has for both men and women. It is related to the

total significance of the college experience and the hope and
promise it has meant for college students through the years.
A few years ago, Roger Wilkins read of the coming Rose Bowl
game between the University of Michigan and the University
of Washington, and this brought back fond memories of his
student days in Ann Arbor and some not-so-pleasant realities
of the present and future. Writing in the *New York Times*, he
recalled those wonderful college days when everyone seemed
full of hope and ambition. Wolverine football teams epitomized
that hope and good feeling as Wilkins wrote:

> Go Blue!
> It's not even a sentence. It has no meaning. And
> yet it means everything. Tomorrow when the Michi-
> gan team races out into the Rose Bowl in its blue
> and gold helmets, its blue jerseys and gold pants, a
> large clutch of partisans who traveled there from all
> parts of the Midwest and up and down California
> will scream: "Go Blue, Go Big Blue Team!"

After relating the excitement and dreams that college and Michigan football represented, Wilkins stated:

> And that is a very large part of what "Go Blue" is
> about. No matter how thick life becomes with fami-
> ly, friends, associates and accomplishments, each
> person's personal freight train becomes more and
> more lonely as it accelerates toward its destiny. One
> good way to understand aging is to know that with
> each passing year, fewer and fewer of the old hopes
> and fantasies that warmed and filled one's youth
> are any longer possible.

He concluded:

> In recent times, in Washington and New York, as
> the years began to rush, I could sense that the
> freight whistle in the night was beginning to mourn
> for me. So hearty with drink and friends, or alone

sometimes, I would yell or cry in silence, as the
Blue Team took the field, for all the slender young
people who used to be, and for all the possibilities
gone.
    So tomorrow, Go Blue! For your glory—and for
mine. For ever and ever. Amen.[23]

With all their vices and complications and irrationalities, intercollegiate athletics appear to be here to stay.

Fund Raising

The significance of Roger Wilkins's statement requires no
further elaboration, and it might be a strong indication of why
some persons contribute large sums of money to their colleges
and universities. While the first intercollegiate athletic competition can be traced to an 1852 crew race between Harvard
and Yale, the concepts of giving and charity in a legal sense go
back to biblical antiquity according to M. M. Chambers. The
idea of charity was accepted by the chancery courts of England
for many years before it attained formal status in the Statute
of 43 Elizabeth (1601). Formal recognition was given to charitable giving because it provided some relief to the government
for such tasks as educating people, treating disease and illness,
and in other ways helping people to survive and become contributing members of society.[24]
    From this beginning current charitable trusts and charitable
corporations have emerged, which have facilitated donations
to colleges and universities, reaching a total of approximately
$3.8 billion in 1979-1980 (see Chapter 4). The activities required
to acquire these donations hold a prominent position in the
operations of both private and public institutions. Fund-raising
efforts are conducted on a continuous basis to obtain support
for operating budgets, and capital campaigns are launched from
time to time to finance the construction of new buildings and
for the major renovation of existing facilities.
    A good fund-raising program is based on the development
of a rational argument that can convince donors that the institution is worthy of their support, although the strong emo-

tional attachments of certain alumni are frequently more important. The rationale for support, or *case* for the institution, should be backed with facts and presented by people who sincerely believe in the institution and are not afraid to ask appropriate individuals for contributions. Many fund-raising authorities stress that leading citizens with wealth enjoy being associated with an important project or worthwhile cause that benefits society in general and their communities in particular.[25]

Fund raising is precise and time-consuming work; it takes a thorough researching of the interests and capacities of potential donors. It requires expert leadership and a real dedication and commitment from volunteers, and it involves matching the right solicitor with the right potential contributor. A dogged but low-key persistence seems necessary, and organization and follow-up are crucial. Persons who contribute substantially to higher education can obtain significant tax advantages. Examination of the different patterns for charitable gifts to colleges and universities indicates some of these benefits. In the first place, a person can make gifts from his or her income or capital, and these gifts can be cash, property, or securities. They can be made on an unrestricted and annual basis for support of current operations, or they can be made for some favorite project of the donor, which is either consistent or changes from year to year. These gifts can also go for capital improvements. Annual giving is the backbone of fund raising, but capital appeals are of equal significance. Both relate to the long-range plans of the institution based on its case for support or "blueprint." The blueprint outlines immediate and long-range goals and opportunities for giving money to support faculty positions, scholarships and student aid of other varieties, construction of, or major improvements to, laboratories, libraries, and classrooms, and similar areas of endeavor.[26]

Gifts that are available for the immediate support of operations and projects are most desirable, but another method of giving has gained importance. This method, deferred giving, includes charitable gift annuities, life income contracts, living trust funds, life insurance plans, and wills providing for direct bequests, bequests with provisions for life income for survivors of the donor, testamentory trusts, or contingent bequests.[27]

Advantages accrue to both the donor and the institution
through tax laws applied to charitable contributions in general
and deferred giving in particular. Specific benefits to donors
can be seen through discussion of four types of life income
plans: charitable gift annuities, pooled life income plans, charitable remainder unitrusts, and charitable remainder annuity
trusts.

Charitable gift annuities can be described by considering the
money or property transferred to the institution as having two
distinct parts. The first part is the actual annuity or the investment in the contract between the donor and the college or
university. It relates to the money to be paid by the college or
university to the donor and is covered by commercial annuity
rates. The second part is the gift itself. When property that is
transferred has appreciated in value over the years, capital
gains taxes are paid only on the annuity part, not on the gift
portion. Since tax laws allow for a charitable contribution
deduction at the time of the transfer, the benefits of that
deduction outweigh the taxes that might be paid on the
capital gain.[28] In general it can be said that the amount allowed
for the charitable contribution deduction is the fair market
value of the property or the money transferred to the college
or university minus the value of the life income interest retained
or in other words, the payment going to the donor.[29]

Pooled life income plans allow a person to give a college or
university a gift of money or property, most frequently long-
term securities which have appreciated in value. These securities
become a part of a fund especially established by the institution
for life income agreement gifts. These pooled funds are then
invested by the college or university, and a donor receives income in proportion to the relationship of his or her gift to the
total fund. For example, if shares in the fund are worth $1,000
each and a person donates $10,000 to a $100,000 pooled life
income fund, that person will receive 10 percent of the earnings
of the fund. When the gift is made, the donor is credited with
a charitable contribution deduction. The amount of this deduction is determined from Internal Revenue Service tables using
the donor's age. If the contribution is large, the unused part
can be carried over into other tax periods up to a maximum

of five years. When the donor dies, the principal of his or her
gift is taken from the fund and used by the college or university
as prescribed in the original agreement. However, the original
agreement can specify income for the lives of a number of
persons. In that case, the principal would be put to institutional
use after the last beneficiary has died. Because gifts are pooled
and because of incentives provided through federal tax laws,
the net income a donor can spend will probably be increased.[30]
Donors are not required to pay capital gains or gift taxes on a
charitable gift in a pooled life income fund. When property is
in the name of the donor alone and provision is made for a
gift to a beneficiary or survivor, gift tax need not be paid if the
donor maintains revocation rights through a will, in other words,
the option of dropping that beneficiary.[31]

The pooled life income plan provides the donor with advantages
as far as federal estate taxes are concerned. The estate includes
the value of units the donor has in the pooled fund with a
charitable contribution reduction recognized for that value.
If the agreement specifies income for the lives of two people
(usually husband and wife) and the donor retains through a
will the right to revoke the survivor's interest, only the value
of the survivor's interest is subject to estate taxes.[32]

Charitable remainder unitrusts provide for a donor receiving
regular payments based on each year's market value of the
trust principal multiplied by the fixed rate selected by that
donor at the time of the original trust agreement. For example,
if a donor makes a gift of $25,000 at the end of the first year
of the trust, the trust is worth $26,500. He will receive the
agreed upon percentage (for example, 8 percent). If in the
second year of the trust it is worth $23,000 the same percentage
will be calculated on the current fair market value of the trust
at that time. In the most widely used type of unitrust, the
donor receives tax advantages because this plan takes into consideration that taxes are applied to five different kinds of
income: (1) ordinary income not distributed in previous years
and the ordinary income for a given tax period; (2) income from
short-term capital gains for the tax year and previous years if it
has not been distributed; (3) income from long-range capital
gains for the current year and previous years if not distributed;

(4) other income from the tax year and other years if undis-
tributed (this includes tax exempt money); and (5) trust principal
money distribution. Considering income at these five levels can
mean lower taxes than if all money is considered as ordinary
income, because losses and gains can be related to specific levels.
Income at all these levels can be distributed on an equal basis to
beneficiaries. If there are taxes, these taxes are applied in the
year that income is distributed. Distribution of income can be
made in total or in part from each level. This type of trust is
not subject to income taxation if debt-financed income is
excluded from it. The trust is also flexible enough to accommodate real estate and stock, which can create special tax
problems in other plans, if the stock is that of a closely held
corporation.[33]

Charitable remainder annuity trusts provide for regular income payments based on a fixed dollar amount. They differ
from the unitrust because the fair market value of the gift is
determined only at the time of the agreement, rather than
every year as in the case of the unitrust. The payment to the
donor is then determined by multiplying that fair market value
by the stated fixed percentage, so that income payments will
be uniform over the years. This amount must be paid by the
college or university without regard for the condition of the
fund.[34]

In addition to the advantages gained by donors through specific plans, in general life income plans free donors from responsibility for the investment of assets. The college or university
and its consultant see to this matter. These plans also prevent
activities in which family members dissipate assets, and they
reduce substantially or eliminate altogether the costs of probating wills. Another advantage is that these arrangements grant
privacy to the donor. In many communities, the probating of
wills is accompanied by considerable publicity, but this does
not apply to deferred giving to institutions of higher learning.[35]

The benefits received by the college or university include
such advantages as knowing that there is an irrevocable commitment to provide the institution with a certain number of
dollars at a given point. Unlike an intention expressed through
an ordinary will or bequest, this commitment cannot be altered
before the death of the donor. Life income plans provide a

college or university with a basis for planning for the future. While the donor receives immediate income tax advantages through a life income plan, the irrevocable nature of that obligation can mean that the donor will take a greater interest in the institution to which that commitment has been made. It can represent a permanent investment of his or her energy and ego.[36]

Tax laws recognize that the special interests of individuals can be served by institutions of higher education if these interests furnish financial support to those institutions for programs and projects they desire. While tax laws change from time to time, they are designed to implement the Internal Revenue Service position that:

> Our federal government recognizes that gifts to religious, educational, charitable, scientific, and literary organizations have contributed significantly to the welfare of our nation; and our tax laws are designed to encourage such giving.[37]

Tax laws, loyalty to the alma mater, nostalgic thoughts of college days, and a number of other factors have contributed to the establishment of patterns of substantial voluntary giving both from individuals and corporations to colleges and universities in the United States. However, the opinion has been expressed that such giving can be increased, even in times of economic recession. George A. Brakeley, Jr., the chairman of the professional fund-raising firm of Brakeley, John Price Jones, Inc., has said that one person out of a total of four hundred in the United States is a millionaire and that the actual number of millionaires is increasing by about 15 percent every year. He expressed the belief that solicitation of funds by organizations and institutions that rely on philanthropic support in 1980 tapped only about one-fourth of the available resources of wealth in this country.[38]

A number of millionaires were involved in two fund-raising campaigns in the 1970s that illustrate the capacity of major universities to gain support of this nature. In 1974 it was announced that Stanford University raised $150 million in the first two years of a five-year campaign to raise a total of $300

million. Of this amount, $125 million was earmarked for endow-
ment, $92 million was for operating expenses, and $83 million
was for capital construction. In the first week of April 1974,
Yale University announced a campaign to raise $370 million
by the end of 1977. Even before this announcement was made,
$63 million had already been raised.[39]

Alumni Relations

Alumni contributed extensively to both the Stanford and
Yale capital campaigns. They have also been consistent donors
to the annual fund. Across the country alumni are responsible
for aproximately one-fourth of all voluntary support for colleges and universities each year.[40] That support is cultivated
while these persons are undergraduate students. The treatment
they receive at that time and the general feelings they have
about the administration, faculty, staff, and their fellow students usually have a marked effect on their attitudes toward
their colleges and universities after they graduate. Just as it
behooves the administration of institutions of higher education
to be open and honest with students, it is also necessary to continue this communication when these students become alumni
and alumnae.

Alumni/alumnae who are satisfied with their colleges and
universities can be invaluable "goodwill ambassadors" as well
as financial contributors and recruiters of students. However,
their loyalty is not automatic. It must be earned by colleges
and universities during undergraduate days and alumni years.
An institution that actively seeks student involvement, provides
an education that equips graduates for society, and maintains
communication after graduation, builds on those nostalgic
feelings discussed by Roger Wilkins. The University of Michigan
is cited frequently for its outstanding alumni association program, which augments tradition with positive action.

Summary

Emotions and feelings play an important role in the decisions
people make and the attitudes they form. In a very real sense,
knowledge held by any given individual relates to that person's

feelings, beliefs, and hunches as well as experiences, observations, and values. The area of institutional advancement, which can include communication and public information, intercollegiate athletics, fund raising, and alumni relations, provides an excellent example of this reality in American higher education. This area is often neglected in scholarly discussion of the organization and administration of higher education. This neglect means that a highly important influence on institutional programs and services has been overlooked. This influence is most difficult to assess in terms of the objective criteria for evaluation that have been established as the ideals for measuring education and accounting to the public for its contribution.

However, that influence must be recognized because of its major impact on all that happens in colleges and universities. Educators and those who are concerned with American colleges and universities need to be honest about the realities at the base of their thinking and action. To neglect the importance of beliefs and emotions in higher education is the epitome of dishonesty.

Notes

1. Thomas E. Jones, Edward V. Stanford, and Goodrich C. White, *Letters to College Presidents* (Englewood Cliffs, New Jersey: Prentice-Hall, 1964), pp. 112-113.

2. Clarence A. Schoenfeld, *The University and Its Publics* (New York: Harper and Brothers, 1954), p. 6.

3. Ibid., p. 3.

4. Howard W. Peckham, *The Making of the University of Michigan, 1817-1967* (Ann Arbor, Michigan: University of Michigan Press, 1967), p. 43.

5. Jack Olsen, "The Black Athlete: A Shameful Story," *Sports Illustrated*, July 1, 1968, pp. 26-27.

6. Lorenzo Middleton, "Teams at 5 Universities Are Penalized for Sidestepping Academic Regulations," *Chronicle of Higher Education*, August 25, 1980, p. 3.

7. George R. LaNoue, "Athletics and Equity," *Change, The Magazine of Higher Learning* 8, no. 10 (November 1976): 27-30.

8. Personal Correspondence, Ilma Z. Wallenfeldt to E. C. Wallenfeldt, November 11, 1979.

9. Lewis Cole, "The NCAA: Mass Culture as Big Business," *Change, The Magazine of Higher Learning* 8, no. 8 (September 1976): 42-46.

10. Kent State University Chapter of the American Association of University Professors, "Memorandum to Faculty: Kent State University; Subject—Minority Statements of the Task Force on Intercollegiate Athletics," mimeographed (Kent, Ohio: Kent State University Chapter of the American Association of University Professors, April 15, 1974).

11. Cole, "The NCAA: Mass Culture as Big Business," pp. 44-45.

12. James W. Long, "Intercollegiate Programs," in *Handbook of College and University Administration: Academic*, vol. 2, ed. Asa S. Knowles (New York: McGraw-Hill, 1970), p. 8:6.

13. LaNoue, "Athletics and Equity," pp. 27-28.

14. National "W" Club, *Wisconsin Vs. UCLA; Official Football Program* (Madison, Wisconsin: National "W" Club, University of Wisconsin, September 22, 1979), p. 41.

15. National "W" Club, *Wisconsin Vs. Michigan State: Official Football Program* (Madison, Wisconsin: National "W" Club, University of Wisconsin, October 13, 1979), p. 41.

16. National "W" Club, *Wisconsin Vs. UCLA: Official Football Program*, p. 41.

17. Robert N. Singer, *Myths and Truths in Sports Psychology* (New York: Harper and Row, 1975), p. 96.

18. George Leonard, "Sports and Competition: Winning Isn't Everything. It's Nothing," *Intellectual Digest*, October 1973, p. 45.

19. Mervin D. Hyman and Gordon S. White, Jr., *Big Ten Football: Its Life and Times, Great Coaches, Players and Games* (New York: Macmillan, 1977), p. 130.

20. Ibid.

21. Lorenzo Middleton, "$287,000 for a Coach Stirs Worry of 'Ripple Effect'," *Chronicle of Higher Education*, February 3, 1982, pp. 1, 9.

22. Tom Wolfe, *Mauve Gloves and Madmen, Clutter and Vine* (New York: Farrar, Straus and Giroux, 1976), pp. 74-75.

23. Roger Wilkins, "An Alumnus Cheers for 'Old Blue,' Long Left Behind but Never Forgotten," *New York Times*, January 1, 1978.

24. Merritt M. Chambers, *Higher Education: Who Pays? Who Gains?* (Danville, Illinois: Interstate Printers and Publishers, 1968), p. 129.

25. John A. Pollard, *Fund-Raising for Higher Education* (New York: Harper and Brothers, 1958), p. 31.

26. Jack R. Bohlen, "The Development Office—Organization, Policies, and Standards," in *Handbook of College and University Administration: General*, vol. 1, ed. Asa S. Knowles (New York: McGraw-Hill, 1970), p. 5:108.

27. Conrad Teitell, "Deferred Giving," in *Handbook of College and University Business Administration*, vol. 1, p. 5:251.

28. Leonard W. Bucklin, "Deferred Giving," in *Handbook of Institutional*

Advancement, ed. A. Westley Rowland (San Francisco: Jossey-Bass, 1977), p. 224.

29. Ibid., p. 214.
30. Ibid., p. 225.
31. Ibid., p. 226.
32. Ibid., p. 227.
33. Ibid.
34. Ibid., pp. 228-229.
35. Ibid., pp. 229-230.
36. Teitell, "Deferred Giving," p. 5:254.
37. Bucklin, "Deferred Giving," p. 218.
38. "Gifts to Higher Education Surpass $3.2 Billion," *Chronicle of Higher Education*, June 9, 1980, p. 9.
39. "Yale Drive Seeks $370 Million: Stanford Reaches Halfway Point," *Chronicle of Higher Education*, April 15, 1974, p. 7.
40. "Gifts to Higher Education Surpass $3.2 Billion," p. 9.

7

ACCREDITATION AND INTERINSTITUTIONAL COOPERATION

Legitimacy for most institutions and programs in higher education requires more than approval and acceptance from the
boards that constitute the offical governing bodies of colleges
and universities. This legitimacy has come about through a
voluntary process in which colleges and universities subject
their programs to a critical examination. This examination is
conducted by personnel from other colleges and universities
according to standards and goals determined by the institutions
being examined and by a "professional" voluntary association
of colleges and universities whose programs and aspirations are
similar to those of the institutions being evaluated. This process
of legitimizing institutions and programs represents a necessary
part of public acceptance of most colleges and universities, and,
in a real sense, it is essential for institutional or program survival
for the majority of institutions of higher education.

Another form of voluntary cooperation has also contributed
to institutional and program survival. In this pattern of cooperation, colleges and universities have worked together through
consortia arrangements to gain benefits and certain advantages
they would not realize acting separately. This chapter discusses
the process of accreditation and national and regional cooperation brought about through the establishment and maintenance
of consortia. Specifically, this discussion involves a consideration
of: (1) the significance of accreditation and professional associations; (2) a definition of accreditation; (3) origins of the
practice of accreditation; (4) the current status of accreditation;
(5) major problems in accreditation; (6) interinstitutional

cooperation—consortia; (7) historical development of consortia and current patterns; (8) governance of consortia; and (9) the status of consortia in recent years.

Significance of Accreditation and Professional Associations

The idea that a person who performs services for members of society should have some official sanction to do so probably received its most significant endorsement in medieval times. The chaos created by barbarian invasions of the Western world resulted in destruction of many customs and practices implemented by Greek and Roman governments. What was retained was the result of the efforts of the church, which provided the sanctions and protections, keeping civilization alive. The church preserved education and led to the establishment of universities, which produced the lawyers, civil servants, clergy, and physicians who gave an order and discipline to human interaction whether that interaction took place at "national" or local levels. The issue as to whether that order was in the best interests of the majority of the people in general or of the specific groups that established it, will remain the subject of debate for centuries. Nevertheless, it was established, and the groups who established it became the certifying agencies for the persons who entered professions. Eventually, professions became organized through associations, and society through its governmental agencies, has recognized these associations as authorities on what is best for people in general when it comes to the services that are delivered by professions those associations represent. Because of this recognition in society, professional associations and accrediting agencies take on an authority that is beyond the formal and legal control exercised by boards of trustees and boards of regents. Herein lies a basic conflict that must be recognized in American higher education, and many plausible conditions in history provide a basis for interpretation. Probably as good as any other explanation is one contending that this nation's leaders have attempted to balance democratic ideals that people should control their destinies in educational realms with a belief in the ability of the expert. It may be a result of a basic belief in the human being's ability, individually and collectively, to make wise decisions and chart directions for the future intelligently. However, this belief is constantly checked because of a tradition of respect for philosopher-kings stemming from Greek ideals and an ever-present need for authority, once divinely, now "professionally," inspired.

A premise seems to apply constantly that people should decide their destinies, but the "expert" is admired and has power to provide direction or intervene in many situations. While boards of trustees and regents have official power, regional accrediting associations and professional groups such as the American Medical Association and the American Chemical Society have attained positions to influence those boards in matters of importance to those associations. These associations determine requirements to be met by students and programs receiving significant funding from both private and federal sources. Their control and influence must be recognized as facts of life.

The importance of accreditation varies from institution to institution and from association to association. In general, regional accreditation of entire institutions appears to be desired by most colleges and universities regardless of institutional prestige. However, should Harvard, Yale, or Princeton decide that regional accreditation is unnecessary, it is doubtful that they would experience any serious difficulty attracting students or research grants, but most degree-granting institutions are regionally accredited.

The matter of accreditation of special programs is another situation. Prestigious institutions have sufficient histories and reputations to make accrediting of secondary importance in many program areas. Lesser known institutions, especially those establishing new programs, place greater significance on accreditation. Societal demands can also influence the status of program accreditation. Demands for persons in various positions in business and industry have meant that a number of colleges of business have functioned for years without being recognized by the American Association of Collegiate Schools of Business. Power and influence vary among professional associations. The American Medical Association occupies the top rung on the ladder and the National Council for Accreditation of Teacher Education is close to the bottom. Relative positions correspond to the status of doctors and teachers in society. The American Medical Association can exercise strong control over college programs while the National Council for Accreditation of Teacher Education is accepted or rejected depending upon the resources and prestige of individual institutions that have programs for the education of teachers.

A Definition of Accreditation

Whether a professional association exercises decisive power or a variety of "friendly persuasion" at most, the process of accreditation is the same. Through this process, an association or agency acknowledges in public that an institution in general or a specific program in particular has met certain standards and requirements designated by that association or agency.[1] The meeting of these standards and requirements has been determined through actual evaluations, either on an initial or follow-up basis.

The ideal model for accrediting has been described as one that encompasses a voluntary application, a self-study, an inspection, and a decision predicated upon the results of that inspection visit. Initially, a college or university applies for accreditation, and this application represents a belief that the institution as a whole or a specific program meets the standards held by the agency. Using these standards, the college or university has undergone an intensive self-study and has submitted the results of this study to the accrediting agency. The inspection phase of the model means that the accrediting agency sends a team of volunteers to make an on-site investigation of the institution or program. The team submits a report to the accrediting agency following its evaluation, and officials of the agency render a decision as to whether the institution or program is to receive initial accreditation[2] or to be continued as an accredited institution, if that initial accreditation has already been granted at some point in the past. The agency can decide that the institution or program does not qualify for initial accreditation, or if the institution or program is being periodically evaluated after initial accreditation, continued accreditation can be denied or extended on a probationary basis.

Origins of the Practice of Accreditation

The United States Constitution leaves the responsibility for
education to the states. New York appears to be the only state
that developed any kind of meaningful accreditation for colleges
and universities. The New York Board of Regents was given
authority in 1784 to act in the manner of a European ministry
of education as the "licensing, regulatory, and planning authority over all educational institutions" whether they were private
or public in terms of support and sponsorship.[3]

The mentality of the expanding western frontier was responsible
for the emergence of many new colleges and universities. The
approach of state authorities to education was similar to that
taken with respect to business, industry, and other elements of
free enterprise. Expansion and growth seemed to be uncondi-
tionally encouraged, and as a result, state government was considerably lenient and permissive with charters for new institutions
of higher education.[4]

However, in contrast to this leniency, the Association of
Collegiate Alumnae maintained a national list of "quality"
colleges and universities for the period from 1882 to 1921. The
association changed its name to the Association of American
University Women (AAUW) in 1921 and as the AAUW continued
to publish this list up to 1963.[5] Another action in the opposite
direction of lenient practices of frontier states was the establishment of standards for institutions of higher learning in New
York in late 1800s.[6]

In 1870 the United States Bureau of Education published a
list of 369 colleges that it recognized, apparently on the basis
that they had been in existence for a considerable period of time
and awarded degrees. This listing proved to be inadequate in
the twentieth century because it was modified only slightly
from its original 1870 form.[7] The Carnegie Foundation in 1905
set up retirement allowances for aging professors and needed
some standards to determine which institutions' professors
were eligible for these allowances. The Foundation used the
standards developed by New York in the late 1800s.[8]

In 1910 the United States Bureau of Education attempted
to refine its list by working with the Association of American

Universities and looking at the graduate program grades of students from various undergraduate colleges. Political complications stopped the publication of this list, which would have classified colleges in four categories from I (qualified) to IV (not qualified). Going back five years from 1910, it should be stated that the University of Berlin in 1905 informed the Association of American Universities "that it would recognize the bachelor's degree of American universities as the equivalent of the German Gymnasium's *Maturitätszeugniss*, but only if taken at a member institution of the Association."[9]

The Association of American Universities accepted American Council on Education standards in 1924, but stopped publishing a national list in 1948.[10]

Accrediting of secondary schools began with the establishment in 1885 of the New England Regional Accrediting Association. It was followed by the founding in 1895 of the North Central Regional Accrediting Association. Eventually problems of articulation between high schools and colleges caused these regional accrediting associations to become involved in the process of accreditation of colleges and universities. The North Central Association became one of the strongest and most rigorous groups because it covered "the Midwest, where populism and public universities were stronger."[11] The spirit of populism reflected the attitude and conviction that people should be protected from vices and evils of administrators and other civil servants who might take advantage of citizens to forward personal gain.

Licensing became the key concept for specialized accreditation. This entailed the idea that the passing of a test to practice a trade or profession was important. The American Medical Association was "the prototype professional association."[12]

The proliferation of accrediting agencies, as more and more professions emerged, necessitated the development of "central monitoring agencies" and principles for agency operations.[13] The National Commission on Accrediting and the Federation of Regional Accrediting Commissions of Higher Education emerged as major monitoring groups. The National Commission on Accrediting developed principles: (1) constructive management of accrediting to reduce costs; (2) self-evaluation of an institution (self-study); (3) evaluation (whether internally or externally accomplished) should consider the entire institution and cover both qualitative and quantitative dimensions; and (4) diversity and autonomy should be preserved as much as possible.[14]

In 1975 the National Commission on Accrediting and the Federation of Regional Accrediting Commissions of Higher Education merged to form the Council on Postsecondary Accreditation. The Council is a private agency, and it serves as a coordinating unit for nongovernmental accrediting functions. It also recognizes accrediting bodies.[15]

The major significance of accrediting agencies in recent years has related to eligibility for federal funding, especially financial support for students. Recognition of postsecondary institutions, whether they are the more traditional nonprofit types or the emerging proprietary schools, by some form of agency for program or institutional accreditation has meant eligibility for students to receive federal funds to finance their education. This eligibility seems to have been abused by some institutions. The existence of some postsecondary institutes and colleges has appeared to rely essentially on the eligibility of students to receive financial assistance from the federal government.

The Current Status of Accreditation

Agencies vary vastly in importance, scale, resources, public standing, influence, and sophistication. Harold Orlans stated in 1974 that these agencies ranged from those that approved hospital "schools" with *no* students to those that were concerned with universities enrolling *40,000* students. Some agencies accredit *no* schools while others accredit 1,000 institutions. Many agencies approve, accept, certify, classify, license, recognize, or register programs.[16]

Seventy agencies were included on a list published by the United States Commissioner of Education in 1979.

> Under law, the Commissioner of Education is
> responsible for publishing a list of nationally
> recognized, reliable accrediting agencies. . . . The
> government uses accreditation as a principal means

for determining which colleges, universities, and vocational schools are eligible for federal aid.[17]

In 1974 Orlans listed fifty-eight recognized accrediting agencies under the following headings:

Higher Commissions—Seven Regional Groups

1. Middle States Association of Colleges and Secondary Schools, Commission on Higher Education
2. New England Association of Schools and Colleges, Commissions on Institutions of Higher Education
3. North Central Association of Colleges and Secondary Schools, Commission on Institutions of Higher Education
4. Northwest Association of Secondary and Higher Schools, Commission on Higher Schools
5. Southern Association of Colleges and Schools, Commission on Colleges
6. Western Association of Schools and Colleges, Accrediting Commission for Senior Colleges and Universities
7. Western Association for Schools and Colleges, Accrediting Commission for Junior Colleges

Other Regional Commissions

1. New England Association of Schools and Colleges, Commission on Public Secondary Schools
2. New England Association of Schools and Colleges, Commission on Vocational Technical Institutions
3. Southern Association of Colleges and Schools, Commission on Occupational Education Institutions
4. The Board of Regents of the University of the State of New York, The State Education Department

Proprietary School Agencies

1. Medical Laboratory Schools
2. Association of Independent Colleges and Schools, Accrediting Commission
3. Cosmetology
4. Trade and Technical Schools
5. Home Study Council

Orlans also listed forty-two Specialized Agencies, examples of which follow:

1. National Architectural Accrediting Board
2. National Association of Schools of Art, Commission on Accrediting
3. Accrediting Association of Bible Colleges
4. National Accreditation Council for Agencies Serving the Blind and the Visually Handicapped
5. American Association of Collegiate Schools of Business
6. American Chemical Society
7. Association of American Law Schools
8. American Bar Association, Section on Legal Education and Admissions to the Bar
9. American Council on Education for Journalism, Accrediting Committee
10. American Medical Association, Council on Medical Education
11. National Association of Schools of Music
12. National Council for Accreditation of Teacher Education[18]

Major Problems in Accreditation

The interests of the private accrediting agencies seem to conflict with broader public interests and public accountability sought by state and federal governments. This conflict appears to be related to the reasoning behind the Newman Committee recommendation of a few years ago that the federal govern-

ment drop accreditation as a basis for eligibility for federal
financial assistance and go to "institutional statements of
disclosure akin to those required of corporations by the Securities and Exchange Commission." [19]

The belief that accrediting agencies are not providing sufficient protection for the consumer seems to have been responsible for other recommendations. Before he left office in July
1979, Joseph Califano, H.E.W. Secretary, recommended that
eligibility for federal financial assistance should rest solely upon
state authorization and not involve institutional accreditation. [20]
A few months before Califano left office an intense debate
took place concerning the role of the federal government in the
accreditation process. The federal government has maintained
a long list of standards and practices that agencies must maintain to be recognized (for example, "clearly defined standards
for institutions they accredit, assure due process in their procedures, foster ethical practices among their members, and
re-evaluate accredited programs at regular intervals"). A proposal
from the Office of the Commissioner of Education called for a
shortening of the list of standards and limiting the agencies
recognized to those that accredit entire institutions. Specialized
agencies would be recognized only when the need arose to
determine eligibility of programs at institutions which were
not accredited. This proposal, which would limit the federal
role in accreditation, was supported by the Council on Postsecondary Accreditation. Council President Kenneth E. Young
stated:

> Accreditation cannot serve as a consumer-protection
> guarantee for more than it attempts to evaluate. It
> cannot, for example, predict which institutions are
> likely to go bankrupt five or ten years from now.
>
> Accreditation cannot, by itself, serve as the basis
> for determining eligibility for federal funds; neither
> can it function as an arm of the government in
> policing compliance with various federal and/or
> state laws and program requirements.
>
> Accreditation cannot allow itself to be used for
> purposes other than evaluating educational quality,

and the burden is always on the accrediting body
to demonstrate that its criteria and procedures are
focused upon that goal.[21]

The Division of Eligibility and Agency Evaluation of the
United States Office of Education took the opposite position
of Young, and the ten higher educational associations which
supported him. The Division expressed the belief that the federal
government should play an even more active role in accreditation
because of the "quasi-public role" accreditation has taken on
in the disbursement of federal funds. Greater scrutiny of accrediting agencies by the federal government is needed, according to Division director, John R. Proffit. Standards and practices
required by the federal government of accrediting agencies
should be increased and agencies should be required to "evaluate
the 'integrity' of the institutions they accredit." Proffit supported his argument with the statement that "recent reports from the
General Accounting Office and the Carnegie Council on Policy
Studies in Higher Education, both" call "for more stringent
review of the activities of accrediting bodies."[22]

The resistance presented by the Division of Eligibility and
Agency Evaluation to the proposal from the Commissioner of
Education in May 1979 apparently was responsible for Secretary
Califano shifting to the position of rejecting accreditation
completely, a position that the Council on Postsecondary
Accreditation finds unsatisfactory.[23]

In the late summer of 1979, the Education Commission of
the States, at its annual meeting, reached the conclusion that:

All states should establish minimum standards for
the authorization and continued operation of all
postsecondary institutions that will protect prospective students from fraudulent practices and
educationally ineffective programs. Standards for
educational operations should be high enough to
assure the citizens and state and federal governments
that all programs provide students a legitimate educational opportunity.[24]

The position of the Education Commission of the States was that licensing by the state was necessary as a precondition for accreditation and the establishment of other voluntary standards and guidelines. According to the Commission, thirty-six states have laws requiring the licensing of degree-granting institutions, but enforcement of laws varies considerably from state to state and many states depend upon the accrediting agencies to "establish minimum standards of educational quality." According to the Commission, institutions to be licensed should show that they are financially sound, that they "can actually provide an educational program at an acceptable level," and that they will present "clear, accurate, and complete information" sufficient to enable prospective students to determine whether or not programs are consistent with their educational interests and meet their needs.[25]

In 1980 the Sloan Commission on Government and Higher Education recommended that all postsecondary institutions, both private and public, be licensed and that "minimum standards, for academic conduct" be set up and enforced to protect the public from deception and fraud on the part of colleges and universities. The responsibility for licensure and enforcement of standards should be assumed by the states.[26]

Program quality would be insured through periodic evaluations of academic offerings of colleges and universities. These reviews would be conducted under the auspices of state boards of higher education and would use regional and special program accrediting groups as much as possible in organization and implementation. The results of these reviews would be published and a response would be presented by the examined institution within one year after the review. Licenses would be granted, renewed, or canceled, depending upon the review. Program reviews would be mandatory for public institutions and voluntary for private colleges and universities.[27] The Sloan Commission has called for licensing because of the need and the responsibility to account for the use of public funds and to keep institutional standards from declining in an economic crisis in which colleges, out of necessity for survival, may recruit and retain students with little consideration for their preparation, ability, and performance.[28]

Another recommendation for the improvement of the process through which institutions and programs are recognized and sanctioned has been made by a special advisory panel in a report to the Council on Postsecondary Accreditation. The panel recommended that the Council be funded directly by institutions rather than by the regional and specialized accrediting agencies whose activities the Council monitors. This recommendation was consistent with the panel's contention that the Council should have more direct contact with individual institutions, and it related to charges that accrediting agencies have imposed "excessive costs and administrative burdens" upon individual institutions.[29]

A member of the Council on Postsecondary Accreditation, President Robert H. Strotz of Northwestern University, applied his knowledge of accreditation goals and practices in a situation on his own campus. This situation provides an illustration of the controversy which has characterized relationships between institutions and accrediting agencies in a number of cases. In 1982 the Accrediting Council on Education in Journalism and Mass Communication was denied information on the salaries of individual faculty members by officials of Northwestern University while the Council was evaluating that institution's graduate program in journalism. President Strotz expressed the belief that such information was irrelevant, and he charged that some of the agencies accrediting specialized programs are less interested in program quality than they are in increasing the salaries and improving work conditions for their colleagues. Representatives of the accrediting group reviewing Northwestern maintained that salary information was necessary to see that there was no discrimination on the basis of sex or race. Officials from the University stated that accreditation really was not necessary because of the journalism school's excellent reputation in the field. There were some other issues in this situation, as there usually are in these evaluations. For example, Northwestern's undergraduate program in journalism did not have accredited status, and questions have been raised about the quality of the graduate program because of the extensive number of credits awarded for internship experiences in the community.[30] However, this example does provide an indication of the controversy related to accreditation.

Clearly, there is a serious question as to whether accreditation practices, procedures, and policies meet the public need to protect consumers and assure that students receive the quality of education they expect. Whether standards are at a bare minimum or indicate a certain degree of quality, measures need to be taken so that the professional's expertise and desire for "quality" can be recognized at the same time that the general public is protected from the special interests of the professional to survive and serve self-interest. This is not an easy assignment, but it is a most important one, since accrediting and licensing agencies, whether they represent a dominance by the state and "public" interests on the one hand or a professional special interest perspective on the other, do exert an influence on higher education of at least equal significance to that brought about by formal boards of control.

Interinstitutional Cooperation—Consortia

Another important influence on higher education has come about as a result of consortia arrangements evolving among colleges and universities in the United States, on which Franklin Patterson has done extensive research and writing. He claims that two guiding principles, cited by a Carnegie Commission, appear to be at the base of consortia planning. The first principle is that cooperation can lead to instructional offerings that are of better quality and greater diversity, and the second is that a greater return can be realized on the dollars invested in cooperative programs.[31]

Research and public service functions provided for society probably should be added to Patterson's principles, so it might be said that desire to provide better instruction, research, and public service at a better price is the reason for consortia arrangements. Actually, any arrangement through which two or more institutions work together might be considered to be a consortium, but Lewis Patterson, another consortia authority, uses more specific criteria in the definition of consortia. He has stated that a consortium must have a voluntary, but formal, organizational structure for its operations, a membership of at least three institutions, arrangements involving a number of academic programs, an administrative staff of one full-time

professional as a minimum, and the requirement that each
institutional member pay a fee to support the operations of
the consortium arrangement as a demonstration of commitment
to its long-range goal.[32]

The healthiest consortia are those with a manageable membership and defined and acceptable goals. Examples are the United
Independent Colleges of Art and the Dallas-Fort Worth Television Intercommunications. However, using Lewis Patterson's
criteria, there were some 31 consortia in 1967, 66 in 1971 (648
colleges and universities being involved), and 80 consortia in
1973 with 797 institutions actually participating. In the fall of
1979, 170 cooperative programs were in existence, involving
775 colleges and universities, or one-fourth of all institutions
of higher education in the United States.[33]

Historical Development of Consortia and Current Patterns

In 1925 the Claremont Colleges of California emerged in a
configuration similar to that of the English institution, Oxford
University. A small group of colleges grew up around Pomona.
Institutional executives and faculty realized that a library and
other academic and support facilities might be used in common
by this group of colleges. The first Claremont College arrangement included the Claremont Graduate School and Pomona
College. Several years later, Scripps College, Claremont Men's
College, Harvey Mudd College, and Pitzer College became
involved. In 1929 some innovative and pragmatic black colleges
developed a basis for economic survival through the establishment of the Atlanta University Center in Georgia. Atlanta
University, Morehouse College, and Spelman College shared
library resources and permitted cross-registration of students,
resulting in a sharing of faculty talents and curricular offerings.
Later, Clark College, the Interdenominational Theological
Center, and Morris Brown College participated in cooperative
arrangements of the Center.[34]

In the 1960s the consortia movement gained additional mo-
mentum as a result of increased enrollments. Colleges and universities were forced to accommodate vast numbers of students,
and they were willing to undertake any number of cooperative

endeavors to do so. Title III of the Higher Education Act of 1965 encouraged cooperative arrangements among colleges and universities. The need for economies in higher education in the 1970s appears to have been responsible for a number of joint-institutional efforts such as the Northeastern Ohio Universities College of Medicine, a venture involving the combined efforts and resources of the University of Akron, Kent State University, and Youngstown State University.

Several years ago, Franklin Patterson provided what he described as a provisional typology of consortia. Included within this typology were cooperative consortia, service consortia, multipurpose consortia, and Title III consortia. In the first category, the best example was the Claremont College pattern of pooling and sharing resources. The most extensively developed model of this type of cooperation has been the Five Colleges, Inc., Consortium, which involves sharing facilities and sponsoring joint academic programs by Amherst College, Mount Holyoke College, Smith College, University of Massachusetts-Amherst, and Hampshire College. In the area of service consortia, a variety of arrangements were described. Single-purpose consortia were represented by the Marine Science Consortium, which was established in 1965 and involved the Pennsylvania State University, state colleges of that state, West Virginia University, and the Catholic University of America. The Marine Science Consortium was established on a nonprofit basis to advance instruction and research in the area of marine science through a utilization of the Wallops Island Marine Science Center in Virginia and a similar center on Delaware Bay. A second classification of the service consortia was provided by the Eisenhower Consortium. This example was a federal research consortium involving nine state universities in Arizona, Colorado, New Mexico, Texas, and Wyoming, and the United States Forestry Service Rocky Mountain Forest and Range Experiment Station in Fort Collins, Colorado. The purpose of this consortium was "to combine and coordinate the research efforts of interested educational institutions and the Forest Service to solve the problems of man and his interventions with the environment."[35]

The multipurpose consortium has been best represented by such arrangements as those of the Associated Colleges of the

Midwest. The Associated Colleges of the Midwest facilitates
cooperation among twelve liberal arts colleges, each of which
provides financial support for the consortium through an annual
assessment and a schedule of fees for participation in individual
programs. Beloit, Carleton, Coe, Colorado College, Cornell
(Iowa), Grinnell, Knox, MacAlester, Monmouth, Lawrence,
Ripon, and St. Olaf College have been members. Associations
like the Associated Colleges of the Midwest have provided
academic services and programs involving off-campus learning
experiences. Arabic studies, Costa Rican development studies,
and Indian studies have been examples of programs it has sponsored. It has also facilitated the provision of banking and library
service for students, a joint admissions and application policy,
and a lobbying office in Washington, D. C.[36]

Title III consortia provisions have pertained to institutions
of higher education that exist in Appalachian Mountain and
inner-city areas, which have been traditionally "isolated from
the main currents of academic life." These institutions have a
greater than normal proportion of low-income students, and
they have received federal funds for faculty development programs, pooled instructional resources, cooperative library
facilities, and coordinated student services. The Kansas City
Regional Council for Higher Education provides a good example
of this type of consortium.[37]

Governance of Consortia

Two tendencies influence governance and decision making.
In the first place, member institutions seem to pursue a course
of action dictated by their individual self-interest regardless of
the general goals of the consortium agreement. In the second,
member institutions tend to allow policy making and decision
making to fall into the hands of the chief executives of the
colleges and universities comprising the consortium. These
presidents, in turn, tend to reflect the tendency of institutions
to act in their own self-interests. These two realities cause the
power of consortium directors to be weak and result in a significant number of consortia representing an ideal rather than
a reality. Most formal consortia have a board of directors con-

sisting of the presidents of the member institutions, usually
with one of those presidents serving as chair. Interinstitutional
committees exist, and sometimes there is a consortium staff.
Presidential commitment and consortium maturity are crucial
to success.[38]

The success of cooperative consortia requires that chief executives of member institutions serve on boards, since they are
the only people who can commit their colleges and universities.
Service consortia usually include many institutions and have
large boards of directors consisting of the presidents of the
member colleges and universities. However, in recent times there
is no service consortium that receives, as institutional support,
more than one-half of 1 percent of the operating budget of any
member institution. Apparently, most presidents have assigned
a low priority to involvement in consortia governance, and
executive directors are required to lead through persuasion
rather than through any kind of actual power. Faculty involvement consists of service on steering committees responsible for
particular consortia programs and acting as on-campus contact
persons for those programs.[39]

In 1974 Franklin Patterson stated that Title III consortia had
a theoretical potential for significant contributions to higher
education because of interinstitutional departments and faculty
appointments, but that three factors were inhibiting the implementation of this "cross-pollinating process." The first was that
distances between participating colleges were too great, the
second that traditional autonomy of institutions stood in the
way of this process, and the third was that funds went to colleges for programs that were cooperative in the theoretical
sense, but not necessarily cooperative in their actual application.
Institutions could actually implement these programs with a
minimum of interinstitutional effort. Because of the extra
initiative and energy required to implement cooperative endeavors, many colleges exerted little effort and did just enough
to qualify for the Title III grants. These funds were viewed as
additional revenue for survival rather than as a basis for real
program improvement.[40]

Patterson's recommendations in 1974 were that "a consortium
needs to determine whether it wishes to be service-oriented or

cooperation oriented" because governance should differ according to purpose.

> The governance of a service consortium should at
> the very least be centralized at the headquarters
> and be directly controlled by those who have the
> highest stake in developing financially viable service
> programs of high quality. This control may be
> realized best by an independent self-governing,
> non-profit or profit corporation contracting to
> serve institutions.
>   . . . the governance of the cooperative consortium
> should be rooted firmly in its participating institu-
> tions.[41]

The board of directors of a cooperative consortium should include chief executives and trustees of the member institutions and extensive participation at the campus level in program decisions and implementation.

The Current Status of Consortia

A study conducted in 1979 by the American Association of State Colleges and Universities in cooperation with the Council for the Advancement of Small Colleges indicated that cooperative programs are on the increase in the United States. Three types of program arrangements seemed to be prominent. The first type concerned seventy-three regional cluster programs related to faculty exchanges, cross-registration of students, joint appointments for faculty, cooperative radio stations and newsletters, and exchanges of residence halls and meal tickets. The study cited the Five Colleges, Inc. as an example of this type of cooperative regional cluster. While this first type was the largest and fastest growing form of cooperation, a second type received recognition. It concerned informal partnerships of two or three institutions and involved faculty and student exchanges, cooperative language study, film festivals, and artists and lecturer programs. Arrangements between Warren Wilson College and Appalachian State University were mentioned. In this context, it was noted that public-private cooperation is increasing at a rate of 5 to 10 percent per year. The third type of cooperation reported was related to special purpose programs. Thirty-two programs were of this nature and pertained to such projects as special interinstitutional interests or unique research facilities, multicampus doctoral programs, a common periodical library service, and shared geology field trips. The Committee on Institutional Cooperation (Big Ten Universities and the University of Chicago) is an organization that works with programs of this type. For all types of programs, the ten activities most frequently mentioned were: (1) cross-registration; (2) coordinated student advising; (3) faculty exchanges; (4) visiting scholars; (5) shared classrooms; (6) joint majors and degrees; (7) library use; (8) faculty development; (9) community events; and (10) lending one institution's administrators to another institution.[42]

Summary

The credibility of colleges and universities requires more than a state charter. A practice has evolved in which approval of programs and institutions by voluntary accrediting associations is necessary to receive federal financial support and assistance from private foundations. There may be some exceptions, but for the most part accreditation is requisite for this support and acceptance from the general public.

Since accreditation is accomplished through procedures involving an evaluation by faculty members from colleges and universities and professionals in the field, the question continues as to whether these persons represent their own special interests or are genuinely concerned with insuring that the public receives the best programs possible. A number of alternatives have been suggested over the years. It is apparent that checks and balances on the special interests of the accrediting associations are necessary. A state licensing procedure in which as many interests as possible are represented appears to have many advantages.

Voluntary interinstitutional cooperation has become an important dimension of many institutional programs. Through cooperative effort, colleges and universities have attempted to provide better programs and services at less expense to individual institutions. Problems have arisen in the achievement of this cooperation because of competition and institutional self-interest.

Regardless of the serious obstacles in attaining the objectives of accreditation and interinstitutional cooperation through consortia, these areas will continue to be of vital concern to educational leaders and all of the interest groups influenced by higher education.

Notes

1. Harold Orlans et al., *Private Accreditation and Public Eligibility* (Lexington, Massachusetts: Lexington Books, 1975), p. 2.

2. Ibid., pp. 2-3.

3. Ibid., p. 7.

4. John S. Brubacher and Willis Rudy, *Higher Education in Transition: A History of American Colleges and Universities, 1636-1976*, 3d. ed. rev. and enl. (New York: Harper and Row, 1976), p. 355.

5. Orlans, *Private Accreditation and Public Eligibility*, p. 15.

6. Brubacher and Rudy, *Higher Education in Transition*, pp. 355-356.

7. Ibid., p. 357.

8. Ibid., p. 358.

9. Ibid., p. 357.

10. Orlans, *Private Accreditation and Public Eligibility*, p. 15.

11. Ibid., p. 9-10.

12. Ibid., p. 11.

13. Ibid., p. 14.

14. Fred O. Pinkham, "The Accreditation Problem," *Annals of the American Academy of Political and Social Sciences* 30 (September 1955): 70-71.

15. Ellen K. Coughlin, "Debate Intensifies over Federal Role in Accreditation," *Chronicle of Higher Education*, May 21, 1979, p. 11.

16. Orlans, *Private Accreditation and Public Eligibility*, p. xviii.

17. Coughlin, "Debate Intensifies over Federal Role in Accreditation," p. 11.

18. Orlans, *Private Accreditation and Public Eligibility*, pp. 114-115.

19. Ibid., p. 52.

20. Harold Orlans, "The End of a Monopoly? On Accrediting and Eligibility," *Change, The Magazine of Higher Learning* 12, no. 2 (February/March 1980): 32.

21. Coughlin, "Debate Intensifies over Federal Role in Accreditation," p. 11.

22. Ibid.

23. Orlans, "The End of a Monopoly? On Accrediting and Eligibility," p. 32.

24. Barry Mitzman, "States Urged to Adopt Minimum Standards for Colleges," *Chronicle of Higher Education*, September 4, 1979, p. 7.

25. Ibid.

26. Sloan Commission on Government and Higher Education, *A Program For Renewed Partnership: The Report of the Sloan Commission on Higher Education and Government* (Cambridge, Massachusetts: Ballinger Publishing, 1980), p. 109.

27. Ibid., pp. 102-104.

28. Harold Orlans, "New Sloan Commission Report: A Program for Renewed Partnership," *Change, The Magazine of Higher Learning* 12, no. 5 (July/August 1980): 45.

29. Robert L. Jacobson, "Bigger Role in Accrediting Asked for College Leaders," *Chronicle of Higher Education*, September 2, 1981, p. 8.

30. Robert L. Jacobson, "Northwestern Denies Faculty-Salary Data to Accrediting Team," *Chronicle of Higher Education*, March 17, 1982, p. 8.

31. Franklin Patterson, *Colleges in Consort* (San Francisco: Jossey-Bass, 1974), pp. 4-5.

32. Ibid., pp. 2-3.

33. "One-Fourth of U. S. Colleges Join Cooperative Ventures," *Chronicle of Higher Education*, September 10, 1979, p. 7.

34. Patterson, *Colleges in Consort*, p. 6.

35. Ibid., p. 14.

36. Ibid., pp. 21-23.

37. Ibid., p. 24.

38. Ibid., pp. 43-44.

39. Ibid., p. 54.

40. Ibid., pp. 54-55.

41. Ibid., p. 62.

42. "One-Fourth of U. S. Colleges Join Cooperative Ventures," p. 7.

8

PUBLIC SERVICE

The idea that education ought to be useful and of benefit to
society at large is at the base of the higher education purpose
of public service. This chapter concerns service and attempts
to examine: (1) extension services and continuing education
as essential components of the concept of service; (2) service
and the urban university; (3) service and the community college;
(4) service and community education; and (5) problems in the
implementation of the concept of service and future directions.

Extension Services and Continuing Education as
Essential Components of the Concept of Service

Extension services have roots in the American lyceum of the
second through sixth decades of the 1800s, the Chautauqua
system of the latter half of that century, agricultural activities
fostered by the land-grant movements of 1862 and 1890, and
the Smith-Lever Act of 1914. They relate to what is now
called continuing education. A broad definition of continuing
education encompasses most of what is regarded as public
service. Jerold Apps states:

> In the broadest sense . . . the purpose of continuing
> education is to enhance the quality of human life
> in all its personal and social dimensions . . . to help
> people acquire the tools for physical, psychological,
> and social survival; to help people discover a sense
> of meaning in their lives; to help people learn how to

learn; and to help communities (society) provide
a more human social, psychological, and physical
environment for their members.[1]

Today extension services are any programs or operations the
institution provides at locations other than its campus, or in
the case of multicampus systems, away from the major campus
of the college or university. Continuing education covers mainly
credit or noncredit instruction for persons in age groups other
than the traditional eighteen to twenty-four year category and
who have educational needs that differ from those of that
traditional age group. When these needs are met at off-campus
sites, they are the objects of extension services. Historically,
the first nontraditional education experiences were through
courses or institutes away from the campus. Hence the relationship between continuing education and extension services was
established, even though today offerings for nontraditional
students are as extensive on the campus as they are at locations
away from that principal instructional facility of many colleges
and universities.

The adult has become an important person for recruitment
in almost all higher education programs, not just the area of
continuing education. Extensive literature on the adult as
learner has appeared over the past decade. Urban colleges and
universities in particular are being directed through state master
plans to cater to the needs of the adult or full-time employee
who wants to improve his or her current position in life through
additional education. This education might mean providing
learning experiences for the accountant who desires Certified
Public Accountant status or making available the opportunity
for a law enforcement officer, willing to dedicate six or seven
years of his or her life to evening study, to attain a law degree.

Noncredit, self-enrichment courses have also become a part
of continuing education. Women's consciousness-raising group
sessions, values clarification workshops, and basket-weaving
and back-packing courses have become dimensions of the offerings of continuing education departments or divisions. A principal reason for all this attention to the adult is the revenue it
might produce. In the early years of the development of extension services in colleges and universities the emphasis may

have been upon the need for an educated and enlightened
citizenry in times of growth and expansion of the western
frontier. Certainly the monetary rewards in terms of increased
tax dollar appropriations from a grateful citizenry were a consideration, but not as they are today. In fact it can be said that
the latest bandwagon in higher education is the education of the
adult student because this is seen as a means to economic survival. Recruitment of nontraditional older students is being
regarded as a measure to offset the decline in the number of
traditional eighteen- to twenty-four-year-old students. The
number of students in this age category is predicted to decrease
by 23 percent by the year 1997.[2]

The question is being raised as to whether increased enrollment of older students can actually offset decline in the number
of traditional students. With the possible exception of some
urban colleges and universities, this is a doubtful expectation,
since older students participate in higher education on a part-
time basis. According to Kenneth Mortimer, higher educational
finance authority, it takes about five part-time adults to produce a credit-hour total equal to that of one full-time traditional
student.[3] That is important because fees are paid and tax dollar
subsidies are received on a credit-hour basis. It should also be
mentioned that many older students may enroll in noncredit
courses which, in most cases for public institutions, do not
qualify for subsidies.

Colleges and universities attempting to attract older students
may not have the human and material resources to meet the
needs of these students. The liberal arts college may not have
the career orientation necessary to help older students develop
new job skills. Faculty at both liberal arts and comprehensive
public and private institutions may lack the ability and experience required to promote the learning of the older student and
may even feel threatened by that person's presence in the classroom. The older student, while initially apprehensive concerning
the "youth culture" environment in the classroom, may be
highly skeptical and critical of the instructor's theoretical and
academic perspective. The task-oriented adult has become accus-
tomed to a world in which gainful employment and productivity
are expected, and his or her learning style is more inclined
toward reflection on personal experiences than is that of the

younger traditional student who tends to be more analytical
and passive.[4]

Institutions should consider carefully their objectives and
resources and the needs and characteristics of adults as learners
before undertaking serious efforts to recruit and enroll older
students. In-service and other faculty development efforts are
probably necessary to reeducate and in other ways help faculty
to understand and teach the adult learner.

Additional consideration should be given to the uncertain
future of a number of aspects of adult and continuing education
in institutions of higher education. Lyman Glenny predicts
that corporations and other types of business firms will find it
more efficient, economical, and relevant to upgrade the skills
of their employees and provide other opportunities for staff
development and continuing education through their own in-
service programs. Functions in these areas of continuing education that have been provided by colleges and universities will
be performed by the companies themselves. Glenny states:

> As the costs of employee turnover increase, industry
> and business, as a fringe benefit, will make renewed
> efforts to educate and train employees on business
> premises, providing internal career ladders for the
> successful, and sharpened skills for others.[5]

Glenny adds a further forecast that could have a definite
influence on adult and continuing education programs in colleges and universities when he concludes that "external agencies,
business and government will do their own examining and licensing rather than relying on colleges and universities for this
purpose."[6]

Part of the endeavor to educate the adult has concerned credit
for life experience. Efforts in this direction face an up-hill
struggle, since educators insist on evaluating this experience in
the same manner that classroom learning is assessed. Paul Dressel
shows insight on this situation when he observes:

> It is inappropriate and even quite unfair to those
> who have acquired an education in a nontraditional
> way to assess that education in terms of acquaint-

ance with traditional materials by the use of traditional evaluation techniques. It is equally unfair to others to accept individually defined objectives and evaluations as the equivalent of traditional courses and degrees.[7]

A major challenge for colleges and universities interested in the continuing education of the adult nontraditional learner is to develop new and more appropriate ways of providing learning experiences which capitalize on that learner's stage of development and background.

Service and the Urban University

The continuing education of the adult and other nontraditional learners is a central concern of colleges and universities located in heavily populated areas. State universities in their expansion and establishment of new campuses have tended to move to centers of population. This has brought about interest in the city university or college on the part of those many persons who support it through tax dollars. The urban universities have been expected to do for the cities what the land-grant colleges have done for the farms. While the public service function was under close scrutiny in the land-grant days of state universities, it appears to be even more closely examined as great expectations have been shifted to the urban state universities. The public service position of state universities has been the subject of considerable criticism over the years. The commitment required by public service to the urban community has been a strain on the American educational system. A sincere involvement of education in the affairs of humankind, while romantic when the United States was thriving on a rural-agrarian economy (and even then strong opposition was raised) seems to have become too grim for scholars as the nation has shifted to an urban-industrial base.

Agricultural extension services and experiments could be performed by farm boys turned professor, who could relate to their clientele because of common roots. However, colleges and universities in an urban environment have not had inner-city blacks, Chicanos, and Eastern Europeans sufficiently accom-

modated by the great American dream to become college professors who could go back to their roots and relate. Even if
such persons had been brought into the system, they may not
have wanted to return to the inner-city in such roles. Their
perceptions of their experiences may not have carried the
nostalgia with which the agricultural extension specialist re-
membered the farm.

As the urban universities came into prominence, college and
university representatives who attempted to relate to the needs
of the inner city had no base for doing so. They have appeared
incapable of establishing the extension co-partnership with
citizens that was possible in agrarian times idealized by the
land-grant concept. They have preached from a pedogological-
authoritarian position instead of approaching problems from
the "fellow-laborer in the vineyard" point of view of the agricultural extension worker. Educators who were responsible for
confronting the problems of the cities seemed reluctant to make
commitments and face the hard realities of the times. Harry
Bard places the situation in perspective when he says:

> Just as the college is part of the joys and rewards
> of the new evolving urban centers, so too it shares
> the cities' problems. It is part of the blood on
> the streets, the confrontations, the dialogue, the
> financial concerns as well as the hopes, the plans,
> the search for a better way. The college in the com-
> munity's midst, cannot run away from these prob-
> lems, for every student who comes from the city
> mirrors these difficulties and brings them into the
> classroom.[8]

J. Martin Klotsche probably has advanced one of the more
realistic positions on the objectives of the urban university. He
has not only attempted to apply the land-grant, public service
concept to the environment of the cities, but he has placed this
concept in a modern perspective for all state universities. He
has asserted in applauding the land-grant service concept that
this praise does not necessarily mean that all aspects of agricultural extension services are applicable to the relationship be-

tween the state university and the city. However, a person
living in the city ought to be able to gain assistance from the
state university in matters related to his or her life as they are
affected by air pollution, sewage disposal, parking and traffic
difficulties, bus service, and consumer prices. In an urban-
industrial society, state universities should be just as attuned
to these problems as they were in earlier times to issues related
to insecticides that would protect crops, the improvement of
soil fertility, livestock strain advancement, and design of farm
buildings.[9]

Klotsche refers to Lyndon Johnson's address at the University
of California at Irvine in June 1964 when the President inferred
that a responsibility of modern universities was to promote
human progress and welfare in the cities in the same way that
land-grant colleges had improved rural life, There are, however,
problems in equating the rural situation with current urban
realities. Communication is more complex in the cities, since
they are complicated sociopolitical organizations in which
many kinds of extension-welfare-public services and programs
are already in operation. University officals need to communicate
with and work with people already providing these services
and programs to avoid unnecessary duplication of effort and
to bring about improvements. Problems of the cities, such as
unemployment, poor health conditions, poverty, crime and
delinquency, drug abuse, and racism, require a well-coordinated
interdisciplinary approach, and solutions that affect, if not
threaten, political and special interest groups. The latter place
conflicting demands and pressures upon universities.

The inner-city situation must be approached in ways different
from traditional methods of education. "Disadvantaged" youth
are a special case in point. However, the needs of these youths
are just one area of consideration in a total approach to urban
problems. Klotsche believes the urban university, to be effective,
needs to make a total commitment involving the entire institution in meeting city needs. Generalists and specialists in many
disciplines must coordinate their efforts in a "team approach."
He cautions that the university that is involved in public service
in the urban environment must continually address questions
about its role:

1. How far can its limited resources be extended
   into the urban field?
2. What activities can be entrusted to other institutions and agencies in the community?
3. What is appropriate for a university to do? [10]

Klotsche cites Abraham Flexner's 1930 statement as a caution
on university involvement in the problems of the cities. Flexner
said, "A university should not be a weather vane responsive to
every variation of popular whim. Universities must at all times
give society, not what society wants, but what it needs."[11] The
university should be selective and exercise judgment in the
types of city problems it undertakes. Institutional involvement
should be consistent with university goals and the human and
material resources the institution has at its disposal. Klotsche's
thinking implies that the university should always be in control
of what it does.

A position similar to Klotsche's is advocated by Solomon
Arbeiter. However, while Klotsche places major emphasis on the
service role of the urban university, Arbeiter even seems to
question whether the university *should* become involved in
service. The community college, he believes, may be in a better
position to provide this service. Like Klotsche, he points out
that conditions in the city today are far different from those
of the rural settings in which most land-grant institutions evolved.
The people to be served are different, and the people who are
to serve their needs must come from a different background
than that possessed by most faculty members today. Arbeiter
believes that the current structure and organization of the urban
university are not suited to meet urban service needs. He states,
"If, however, the university because of political or ultruistic
motivations does wish to serve an urban constituency, then
for that portion of its service, it must reorder its priorities,
reward structure, internal incentives, and educational and
credentialing processes."[12] People should be employed who
may not have the traditional academic credentials, but have
special skills in relating to "disadvantaged" students. Ability
to work in community development situations should be
considered more important than research and other traditional

skills, and that community development ability should have a
top priority in the reward system. Arbeiter states:

> In the realm of urban service, such a university
> would be much more proficient in dealing with urban
> problems, as it could much more easily involve its
> faculty members and students in the full spectrum
> of community life. Attainment of specific skills by
> students would enable them to join community
> projects, governmental units, and business concerns.
> The skills they obtained would be melded to the
> different community needs, and these, in turn,
> would be used in developing and revising courses
> and curricula at the university.[13]

Evidence can be found to indicate that universities situated
in urban settings have not made those changes advocated by
Klotsche and Arbeiter. Walter Waetjen, after serving as President
of Cleveland State University for five years, mentioned the
need to make a thorough study of the structure and organization
of his institution to determine its adequacy in meeting urban
needs. He stated that "CSU isn't organized any differently
from a university in the boonies. If this is an urban institution,
are there ways of organizing that permit us to address urban
problems?"[14]

Waetjen's concern over a total commitment of the University
related to his statement that Cleveland State University's Institute of Urban Affairs, while an important component of the
institution, might be used by faculty not directly working with
the Institute as an excuse not to become involved in urban issues.
Commenting on the creation of urban affairs departments, institutes, or colleges, Waetjen said, "There is a tendency when you
do that for other faculty to say, 'we don't have to be concerned
with urban matters because that's what they do over there.'" He
also expressed the belief that it was a fallacy to consider academic research and urban service as two distinct functions.
The two areas go together because "the best way to get at
urban problems is through research."[15]

In spite of the failure of urban faculties to see the connection
between research and urban service, and even though most

universities are not organized to do so, some progress has been
made in addressing urban problems. An example of an institution
in an urban setting taking on an urban problem is Johns Hopkins
University and its involvement in the Greater Homewood
project. Financed through funds from Title I of the Higher
Education Act, this project saw University faculty working
with citizens in the Homewood neighborhood of northern
Baltimore. The faculty, from 1967 through 1969, helped the
neighborhood define problems, determine possible resources,
develop community leadership, and devise the methods through
which community action programs could be implemented.
The project resulted in the development of a community master
plan, more adequate enforcement of housing, health, and zoning
codes, solutions for some traffic problems, improved schools,
encouragement to appropriate businesses and social services to
come into the area, and the organization of a citizen-controlled
nonprofit association to deal with programs on a continuing
basis. Community development projects of a similar nature
have been successful in Syracuse and St. Louis. Programs directed toward service to individuals appear to be more numerous
because their implementation does not require the time, coordination of effort, and community support necessary for
community development programs. An adult career education
program using television, radio, and newspapers to reach disadvantaged and difficult to contact adults provides a good
example of individually oriented services. This program, cen-
tered in Madison, Wisconsin, was sponsored by a fourteen-state
consortium and some Canadian universities.[16]
   Numerous examples of programs of this nature might be
cited, but there appear to be few programs that show a total
institutional, coordinated, and interdisciplinary approach combined with extensive community involvement. This kind of
community development approach, requiring actions and conditions specified by Klotsche and Arbeiter and implied by
Waetjen seems rare indeed in American higher education.

Service and the Community College

   One reason why urban universities have not restructured,
reorganized, and restaffed to address the problems of the cities

more adequately might be the existence of comprehensive community junior colleges in most metropolitan areas. These two-year institutions have come to regard community service as a most important function. While the main reason for the establishment of public junior colleges was to provide the first two years of higher education as an extension of the public secondary school system,[17] they expanded to cover the realm of occupational and vocational training and took on the function of meeting the educational needs of all members of their communities regardless of needs, interests, and backgrounds.[18]

These functions were specified in a statement of the Accrediting Commission for Junior Colleges of the Western States Association. In formulating general guidelines for standards in community service in 1966, the Association established an elementary language that appears to have been adopted by most community colleges in their official publications. Association guidelines refer to educational services, cultural and recreational services, and the use of college facilities. Educational services are defined as (1) non-credit short courses, seminars, workshops, institutes, conferences, symposiums; (2) leadership in community research and development; (3) community counseling and consultative services; (4) use of radio-television stations; (5) provision of faculty and student programs for community groups.[19]

Activities encompassed within these guidelines have come to include: programs for the aged and culturally, socially, and economically disadvantaged; counseling for alcohol and drug abuse, death, divorce, job loss, and other personal crisis; consumer education; personal health education; and cross-cultural information to promote understanding, appreciation, and tolerance of diverse cultures. Also emerging have been planning, evaluating, and problem-solving endeavors undertaken to assist agencies, groups, organizations, associations, or individual persons in the community. Schools, voluntary associations, clubs, governments, industries, or businesses are objects of services.[20]

The concept of community services has been expanded to cover community improvement and renewal, and this idea emphasizes the requirement that personnel of the college work closely with individuals and agencies within the community.

It is believed by some that universities and college
past have delivered the kind of services they though
portant, and these services have tended to be of a t
nature. Little attention has been given to what the
in the community think is needed, and communit'
have not been developed to the extent that is pos:
full potential is considered. Institutions, although
an interest in community services, all too frequer
programs that are "essentially campus-based and
oriented." It is argued that:

> The time has come to look beyond the cor
> of extension service, community schools, (
> nity service, and community-based education wnicn
> has presumed their goal to be responsiveness to the
> learner and the community. What is needed now is
> a goal that includes not just responsiveness to needs
> but leadership in the improvement of all aspects
> of community life. Beyond being community-based,
> our colleges must now aim at human and commu-
> nity renewal.[21]

This requires identifying those served, plans to overcome barriers,
and flexible methods, programs, and services.[22]
Human and community renewal advocates recognize that
four-year colleges and universities are examining and evaluating
their roles with respect to the communities in which they are
located. The question is being raised: "How does the local
community college, operating next door to such a senior institution, coordinate with that institution when trying to fulfill
community needs?"[23]

Service and Community Education

A further question regards the relationship of four-year and
two-year institutions to community education, another important development that has been brought about by the idea
that education should be more attuned to changing social
conditions and needs that have emerged as a result of these
changes. This development, while it relates more directly to

the public schools, has a significant connection with the service
role of community colleges and four-year institutions of
higher education. The concept of community education, through
which the public school was seen as an agency for meeting the
educational, recreational, and cultural needs of adults in the
neighborhood as well as providing education for children and
youth, evolved initially and indirectly from the effort of Horace
Mann, Henry Barnard, Caleb Mills, and others in the nineteenth
century. These people believed public schools should be reformed
to meet emerging societal needs.[24]

The 1929 stock market crash and the subsequent depression
meant that resourcefulness and reliance on neighbors were
important elements of survival, and the local community became
a focal point for these endeavors. Samuel Everett spoke of the
community school as the center for neighborhood problem
solving in the 1930s. Over the years, community development,
adult education, and recreation needs have been the concern of
community education centers focusing primarily on the public
school as the facility for the delivery of services and programs.[25]

More recently the movement has extended beyond the school
building and has encompassed consideration of all appropriate
agencies and facilities in the community. A grass-roots approach
has been fundamental to the movement with democratic involvement of concerned persons and an attitude of helping people to
help themselves representing vital components. Today, the
community education director functions as a coordinator for
the delivery of services, working in cooperation with other
agencies and persons to meet community needs. Differences
of opinion appear to exist as to the extent of the needs the
community education concept embraces. In some areas this
seems to be limited to adult education and recreation, while in
others, extensive community development programs are concerns
in addition to strictly adult education needs.

Regardless of the difference in degree with respect to the
implementation of the community education concept, it is a
significant factor in the area of community and public services
that should be incorporated into any program of services considered by colleges and universities. Since the service objectives
of community education and the desire of comprehensive community junior colleges to serve the needs of their immediate

environments run parallel, mutual recognition and cooperation
are important. A number of efforts have been made at the
national level to bring about this cooperation. Communication
between the National Community Education Association (NCEA)
and the American Association of Community and Junior Colleges
(AACJC) was implemented on a continuing basis in 1975
through the establishment of the Center for Community Education
by the AACJC.

The AACJC has been involved in a number of discussions and
deliberations of national organizations concerned with communication and cooperation among agencies providing community
education. The first of these sessions involved the NCEA, the
American Association for Leisure and Recreation, and the
National Recreation and Park Association, and it was held in
Flint, Michigan, in 1974.[26] Guidelines for cooperation were
developed as a result of this meeting, and a second meeting was
held in 1977 with the associations involved in the first session
being joined in their deliberations by the National Association
of Public and Continuing Adult Education and the Adult
Education Association of the United States of America. In the
summer of 1977, a national joint position statement was issued
by all five of these associations, stressing that the associations
had goals in common and should communicate and cooperate
in the best interests of those whose needs they desired to serve.[27]
The AACJC joined these five associations in 1980 in issuing
another statement, a major emphasis of which was the recommendation that:

> . . . all communities and states engaged in commu-
> nity education establish a strong formal system of
> interagency communication, coordination, and
> cooperation between and among education,
> recreation and park, and other community serving
> systems. This would provide for the joint planning,
> development, and operation of programs, facilities,
> and services and would aid in preventing duplication.[28]

It appears that four-year colleges and universities have not been
involved in these efforts to cooperate at the national level. Their
major continuing education association, which is the National

University Continuing Education Association, has not participated in any of the meetings and cooperative efforts which
have been discussed. This might raise the question as to whether
community education leaders desire extensive involvement from
four-year institutions, or whether university and four-year
college personnel are interested in cooperating with other
agencies.

One of the few efforts at national level cooperation between
four-year public service people and community educators was
a 1977 conference on community education and cooperative
extension held at Blacksburg, Virginia. Out of seventy participants, only five represented community colleges, and thirteen
were from state universities.[29]

Commitments to cooperate made by associations at the
national level might be subject to challenge. What is professed
at that level may not be consistent with practices of local institutions and agencies. Special interests and needs for survival
on the part of these institutions and agencies take precedent
over those "noble" commitments. The proof of cooperation
is at the local level, and there is evidence that cooperation has
occurred. For example, a 1974 survey of 900 community
colleges revealed that, of the colleges offering off-campus
courses: (1) 84 percent cooperated with local public schools;
(2) 64 percent worked with public schools in the planning of
programs; and (3) 23 percent shared expenses with public
schools.[30]

However, cooperation among community schools, community
colleges, and four-year institutions of higher education remains
suspect. In fact, there are even instances in which state legislators
have withheld financial support for adult education and related
services until community schools, community colleges, and
state universities cooperated in the development of a plan recognizing the contributions, resources, and roles of each of the
three types of institutions in a coordinated effort.[31]

Special interests and survival needs of four-year institutions,
community colleges, and community schools may impede
cooperation. It may be that constituents, the communities and
people whose needs are to be served, must force greater cooperation. This will require an understanding of politics and the
pragmatic implications of special interests. As a start, the lack

of involvement of American higher education's most prestigious
institutions, the state universities, in discussions of community
education-community service cooperation at the national level
should be questioned.

Problems in the Implementation of the Concept of Service and Future Directions

When the problems of the cities can no longer be ignored and
educational institutions start asking some fundamental questions,
the interest of persons and groups in positions of power surface
and some rather threatening situations may arise for those persons
and groups. A board of trustees member may find that his financial
interests in the inner city are endangered by consumer advocacy by
university professors. Attacking city problems, conducting applied
research, and attempting to promote human welfare might, therefore, have a negative influence on the survival of an institution
whose professors exercise that academic critical inquiry prerog-
ative. This is a reality understood by many but infrequently
expressed directly as a reason why certain areas of inquiry might
be off limits for colleges and universities. In subtle ways, it may
even be related to a faculty reward system, which seems to
place little value on service and applied research.

Presidents can expound the virtues of a commitment to a
service role in society. C. Peter Magrath, President of the University of Minnesota, states that "the demands for research and
service are certain to surpass our current capabilities and this
fact will demand an effective and convincing lobbying campaign."[32] Magrath implies that service should be emphasized;
yet, a few years ago Metropolitan State University was created
to attend to the service needs of Minneapolis-St. Paul, the
twin-city area in which the University of Minnesota is located.
Apparently the University of Minnesota had more important
national and international missions, which precluded its attending to problems of its immediate neighborhood. What
would happen to the national and international missions of
the University should Minneapolis and St. Paul deteriorate to
the extent that the University could no longer function in that
locale?

Harold Enarson has pointed out:

Unquestionably, some urban universities have been
bad neighbors, have been uncomfortable in dealings
with the poor and especially with blacks, have
studied poverty in Venezuela rather than a mile
away, have been largely indifferent to glaring problems nearby. The record is not good.[33]

However, he indicates that problems of the cities are complex
and should also be the concern of institutions other than those
located directly in the urban setting. The distinction between
an "urban-oriented" and a "rural-oriented" university is false
and inappropriate when considering major universities in America today. He cites the fact that many land-grant universities are in metropolitan areas at present because of the
phenomenal growth of the communities in which they were
originally established. He looks at these institutions and concludes that "their interests, as they should be, embrace the
full range of human inquiry."[34]

   Enarson's approach provides for a broad involvement of state
universities in the affairs of humankind. Solomon Arbeiter
implies directly that community colleges rather than state universities may be in a better position to solve the problems of
the cities. Arbeiter's stand can be attacked vigorously when
consideration is given to the needs of America's cities and the
capability of community colleges to meet these needs. Community colleges can teach and they have the capacity to counsel,
but their research powers are hardly adequate to examine major
problems in cities. Walter Waetjen, it will be recalled from previous discussion, has said that "the best way to get at urban
problems is through research." The research capability of the
community college is subject to some very important questions.
In 1972 Robert McCabe and Cynthia Smith presented a report
that seems to have significance when the role of the community
college in conducting research is evaluated. This report was
based upon reactions from seventy-two community-junior
college faculty leaders and administrators to a list of nineteen
skills, competencies, and attitudes preferred in teachers. Dem-
onstrated research proficiency in a discipline was given the
lowest rating. This raises the question as to whether community
colleges actually have interest in conducting research that might

find answers for some fundamental problems in both urban and
nonurban areas. Do the community colleges really attract faculty
who are interested in urban problems and do the people that
community colleges employ actually have the background and
ability required to do research in the areas of crime, delinquency,
unemployment, city planning, transportation, consumer economics, drug abuse, urban flight, administration of welfare services,
and other problem areas where solutions are so vital to the
survival of American cities? [35]

The research capability that community colleges do possess
may be so completely consumed by federal and state compliance
requirements that it has little time for attention to community
problems. The detailed reports required by agencies of the state
and federal governments, because community colleges rely
heavily on funding from these sources, may mean that the
personnel of institutional research offices spend an inordinate
amount of time collecting data in compliance with county,
state, and federal regulations. Extensive computer time is
consumed by programs related to these reports. The magnitude
of paperwork required to meet county, state, and federal requirements is almost incomprehensible. Federal regulations,
which numbered 25,000 in 1974 alone, required 5,146 different
reports in just that one year. It was reported in 1977 that
Brevard Community College in Florida, during the period of
approximately one month, was required to complete fifteen
federal report forms, thirty-one state reports, and nine county
reports. [36]

This example not only shows how costly county, state, and
federal requirements are in terms of human and material resources, but it also points out that valuable institutional research
and computer time is being consumed. This time might be
much better spent on studies of community problems. However,
even if the staffs now doing institutional research in community
colleges were "freed up" to direct their attention to social,
economic, and educational problems, serious questions about
their ability to conduct necessary research might be raised.
Reports on the use of government funds and compliance with
regulations do not require the skills necessary to investigate
complicated community social, political, economic, and educational problems. In other words, community colleges can

hardly be expected to "save" the cities all by themselves.

If the resources of universities and colleges are to be used in attempts to solve urban problems, the actual activities to which these resources are now being committed should be considered. In 1978 the results of an extensive survey by the Community Education Division of the AACJC concluded that diverse offerings were available, but that more could be done to serve larger numbers of people. However, the questionnaire used in this survey, sent to 855 colleges, contained not one item on research and development in the improvement of human services nor to the solution of problems of unemployment, crime, delinquency, transportation, or city planning.[37] This survey was supposedly concerned with community service, but it is apparent that research and development activities were not an important consideration. Are community colleges really interested in research and development related to social, political, and economic problems?

If research is important in confronting these problems, it would seem that the best talent available should become involved, and this means a commitment on the part of major research universities. This commitment to the resolution of complex social, political, and economic problems of American society from major research universities is obviously lacking.

The ideal, if the interests of a broad range of people are to mean anything, implies a commitment from these universities and more cooperation among community education, community college, and university leaders. In times of economic decline, greater cooperation may be too much to expect when recognition is given to politics, power, and special interests. However, if the ideal is pursued, the community education director may be in the best position to serve as the person who coordinates efforts and brings a wide range of services to bear on the problems and needs of a specific community. This person may be in the best position to view problems from the perspective of the people in the neighborhood as a special interest group in itself and not from the position of special interest groups such as educational institutions and service agencies. This individual can serve as liaison with the colleges, universities, and any other agency or organization possessing the needed problem-solving resources.

Task forces of specialists from these institutions, agencies, and organizations can work with local citizens in arriving at solutions for community problems.

In essence, this is what community education directors are already doing in more progressive communities. They are not aligning themselves with any particular institution or agency, but are attempting to approach problems with the best interests of the people in the neighborhood at heart. There is, however, a problem with the community education movement as it is currently viewed. This may not actually be a problem in those communities in which the public schools are trusted and supported. In the majority of situations, it appears that the public schools and their boards may not have this trust and support. Strikes and failures to pass levies seem to provide relevant evidence for this belief. The role of the community education director must be expanded, so that this person can become the modern counterpart of the rural county agent created by the Smith-Lever Act of 1914. The idea that the position of the county agricultural agent might be used as a basis for new relationships in urban-industrial times is certainly not new. However, much more attention to this concept as it relates to the role of the community education director appears necessary. The base of operation for this person must go beyond the public school system, both in reality and in the minds of the public, to provide for broader influence and support. A combined status and funding might be developed involving school district, county, state, and federal support, depending upon the size of the community being served.

The education of the community education director would have to be expanded from its current public school orientation, and special efforts should be made to recruit potential directors from as diverse a range of life-styles and backgrounds as possible to meet the needs of the wide range of neighborhoods and communities in America.

This idea requires thorough consideration, and it must be studied from as many perspectives as possible before it can be taken seriously. However, it does seem to allow for an incorporation of the best from the community school movement, the land-grant tradition, the extension idea, and notion of

human and community renewal. It is based on a belief in the
people.

The politics of special interest groups and a number of other
realities in American life can be discouraging and depressing in
terms of an idealized concept of what is best for the people, but
belief in the people always seems to be a romantic and exciting
ideal that helps the country rally from setbacks and disappoint-
ments. In the 1940 motion picture, *The Grapes of Wrath*, the
last words are spoken by Ma Joad as the family was driving from
a migrant worker camp after experiencing personal tragedy,
hardship, and defeat. The Joads were moving on in anticipation
of new jobs and better opportunities in the bitter times of the
Depression. As they drove down the road in their dilapidated
Model T Ford truck, Ma said:

> . . . But we keep a-comin'. We're the people that
> live. Can't nobody wipe us out. Can't nobody lick
> us. We'll go on forever, Pa. We're the people.[38]

Summary

The public service function in American higher education
had its origins in the days of the expansion of the western
frontier and the movement to popularize knowledge and apply
it to the problems of society. The American lyceum, the
Chautauqua system, the Morrill Acts of 1862 and 1890, and
the Smith-Lever Act of 1914 provided the principal impetus
that spread educational programs and services to all corners
of the states. In recent times, the adult student has become
an important object for extension services, which are now
referred to as continuing education. Caution should be exercised in this area, since not all colleges and universities are
equipped, as far as both resources and philosophy are concerned,
to meet the needs of older students.

An argument can be made that the service function of universities has declined in terms of efforts to solve the many difficult problems of the cities, perhaps as a result of complicated
political situations and special interests. Research efforts are in
other safer directions, which mean greater rewards for faculty.

Another reason for the lack of university involvement in the solution of community problems may be the expectation that community colleges should be responsible for this area. However, the limited research resources of those colleges raise serious questions about this expectation.

Any effort to provide community or public service should take into account the community education concept that centers on the neighborhood school as the facility for meeting community educational needs and advocates the participation of people and the coordination and delivery of services through a community education director. Cooperation among the many agencies, including but not limited to state universities, community colleges, and community schools, which are concerned with services to individuals and groups in the community, is essential but has been lacking on any large scale. Competition and special interests of agencies have impaired this cooperation. One solution may be to concentrate on the neighborhood as a special interest group in itself and to provide a mechanism through which that interest group's needs can be considered as foremost. A community education director, responsible to the people of that neighborhood or community but with official status at both a community college and a state university as the principal leader for community service is worth considering. This notion incorporates the best of American ideals.

Notes

1. Jerold W. Apps, *Problems in Continuing Education* (New York: McGraw-Hill, 1979), pp. 91, 101.

2. Malcolm G. Scully, "Carnegie Panel Says Enrollment Decline Will Create a 'New Academic Revolution,'" *Chronicle of Higher Education*, January 28, 1980, p. 11.

3. Jack Magarrell, "The 1980's: Higher Education's 'Not-Me' Decade," *Chronicle of Higher Education*, January 7, 1980.

4. J. Conrad Glass and Richard F. Harshberger, "The Full-Time, Middle-Aged Adult in Higher Education," *Journal of Higher Education* 45 (March 1974): 211-217.

5. Lyman A. Glenny, "Demography and Related Issues for Higher Education in the 1980's," *Journal of Higher Education* 51 (March/April 1980): 377.

6. Ibid.

7. Paul L. Dressel, "Models for Evaluating Individual Achievement," *Journal of Higher Education* 51 (March/April 1980): 205.

8. Harry Bard, "Communicating With Local Government Officials: As the President of the College Sees It," *Community and Junior College Journal* 44, no. 4 (December/January 1974): 32.

9. J. Martin Klotsche, *The Urban University* (New York: Harper and Row, 1966), p. 51.

10. Ibid., p. 56.

11. Ibid.

12. Solomon Arbeiter, "Point of View: Urban Universities Won't Work Unless . . . ," *Chronicle of Higher Education,* April 15, 1974, p. 20.

13. Ibid.

14. "CSU to Study Urban Approach," *Cleveland Plain Dealer,* February 5, 1978, Sec. 1, p. 16.

15. Ibid.

16. George E. Spear, "The University Public Service Mission," in *Universities in the Urban Crisis,* ed. Thomas P. Murphy (New York: Dunellen Publishing, 1975), pp. 97-101.

17. Win Kelley and Leslie Wilbur, *Teaching in the Community-Junior College* (New York: Appleton-Century-Crofts, 1970), p. 8.

18. Ibid., p. 12.

19. William A. Keim, "A Dynamic Definition of Service," in *Reaching Out Through Community Service,* ed. Hope M. Holcomb (San Francisco: Jossey-Bass, 1976), p. 6.

20. John M. Nickens, "A Taxonomy for Community Services," in *Reaching Out Through Community Service,* ed. Hope M. Holcomb, pp. 13-17.

21. James F. Gollattscheck, Ervin L. Harlacher, Eleanor Roberts, and Benjamin R. Wygal, *College Leadership for Community Renewal* (San Francisco: Jossey-Bass, 1976), pp. 5-6.

22. Ibid., pp. 136-137.

23. Ibid., p. 121.

24. Maurice F. Seay et al., *Community Education: A Developing Concept* (Midland, Michigan: Pendell Publishing, 1974), p. 20.

25. Ibid., p. 21.

26. National Joint Continuing Steering Committee Representing the National Community Education Association, American Association for Leisure and Recreation, and National Recreation and Park Association, *The Ultimate—To Serve . . . Through Interagency Communication, Coordination, and Cooperation Between Parks and Recreation and Community Education* (Arlington, Virginia: National Recreation and Park Association, 1976), pp. 3-4, 7-8, 13-19.

27. National Joint Continuing Steering Committee, *Beyond Competition* (Arlington, Virginia: National Park and Recreation Association, 1977), pp. 1-2.

28. National Joint Continuing Steering Committee on Continuing Education, *A National Initiative on Interagency Cooperation: The Ultimate—To Serve II* (Arlington, Virginia: National Park and Recreation Association, 1980), p. vii.

29. Virginia Polytechnic Institute and State University, *Proceedings, National Conference on Community Education and Cooperative Extension* (Blacksburg, Virginia: Virginia Polytechnic Institute and State University, 1977).

30. Eugene E. DuBois and Sandra Drake, "The State of Cooperative Relations Between Community Colleges and Community Schools," *Community Education Journal* 5, no. 1 (January/February 1975): 10.

31. Edmund J. Gleazer, Jr., "A Significant Linkage," *Community Education Journal* 5, no. 1 (January/February 1975): 6.

32. Magarrell, "The 1980's: Higher Education's 'Not-Me' Decade," p. 9.

33. Harold Enarson, Review of *The Urban University in America* by Maurice R. Berube, *Journal of Higher Education* 51 (January/February 1980): 104.

34. Ibid., p. 105.

35. Robert McCabe and Cynthia M. Smith, "New Programs and Practices and Desirable Faculty Competencies and Attitudes," in *Graduate Education and Community Colleges*, ed. S. V. Martorana, William Toombs, and David W. Breneman (Washington, D. C.: National Board on Graduate Education, 1972), pp. 12-14.

36. Louis W. Bender and Robert L. Breuder, "The Federal/State Paperwork Menace," *Community College Review* 5, no. 1 (Summer 1977): 17-18.

37. Robert B. Young, Suzanne M. Fletcher, and Robert R. Rue, *Directions for the Future: An Analysis of the Community Services Dimension of Community Colleges* (Washington, D. C.: American Association of Community and Junior Colleges, 1978), pp. 6, 49.

38. Tom Stemple, *Screenwriter: The Life and Times of Nunnally Johnson* (San Diego: A. S. Barnes, 1980), p. 3.

9

PLANNING AND EVALUATION

Planning theory has a historical basis in rationalistic philosophy, which can be traced to the ancient Greeks. The dialogues
of Plato and the logic of Aristotle emphasized reason and order.
Centuries later Peter Abelard emphasized reason and inquiry
over divine authority and faith. René Descartes echoed Abelard's
sentiments five hundred years later, and Abelard's position
might very well have been the recipe for the Scientific Revolution.[1] Descartes assumed that all people had the capacity to
reason and make correct judgments, but he emphasized that the
application of a method of critical analysis was necessary to
discover the truth.[2] In modern times, the analytical philosophy
of Bertrand Russell and Alfred North Whitehead and the logical
positivism of Ludwig Wittgenstein and the Vienna Circle have
advanced the idea that symbolic logic and mathematical reasoning are principal methods for the advancement of knowledge.[3]

   The scientific method has been advocated for academic pursuits
in colleges and universities for centuries. However, its application
to management problems in higher education has been much
slower in coming. Consideration of planning for the present
and future and the evaluation of programs and services which
emerged through this planning did not gain a significant priority
until business and industrial concepts of marketing, advertising,
promoting, and product performance were acceptable to colleges
and universities. All of these concepts can be incorporated in
the application of the scientific method to higher education
management responsibilities. A broad consideration of the
scientific method includes steps that call for a definition of the

problem for which a solution is being sought, observation and consideration of all factors and conditions that relate to the problem, development of a hypothesis or hypotheses which constitute a hunch or hunches concerning the appropriate solution, and an actual testing of hypotheses or hunches under controlled circumstances in which accuracy of hypotheses or hunches can be determined.[4] This should be kept in mind as this chapter: (1) describes the planning process; (2) discusses futures research; (3) relates planning to evaluation through an examination of the three management techniques of planning, programming budget systems (PPBS), zero base budgeting (ZBB), and management by objectives (MBO); and (4) discusses methods of evaluation.

Planning

George Steiner emphasizes that planning is an integral part of the duties and functions of all managers regardless of their level of operation. He makes distinctions between planning at various levels of management, and these distinctions relate to his rationale for differentiating between levels of management. Steiner speaks of the highest level of management in an organization as being "strategic" management with other levels given the designation of "operational" management. Strategic planning is a process that outlines the overall objectives, directions, and limitations for operational management. While it is certainly concerned with operations, it stresses strategy. The complications of constantly changing conditions in the business environment have meant that organizational survival depends upon the ability to adjust quickly in response to changes both inside and outside the organization. Management must go beyond efficient utilization of limited resources in the manufacturing of goods or production of services at prices people are willing to pay in a current market. Profit in present times depends upon much more than this. The future and preparation for it must be major considerations.[5]

The expression "strategic" has been taken from the language of the military and relates to warfare. Steiner's reference to "operations" or "operational" really means "tactics" or

"tactical" in this context. When the military-warfare analogy
is used for the planning of a business or educational endeavor,
the crucial nature of strategy can be realized. A good overall
strategy can overcome tactical errors. Battles might be lost,
but wars can still be won, because strategies can include con-
tingencies and allow for calculated risks.

Strategic planning requires top-level managers to consider the
goals of their organizations, the human and material resources
they have at their command and work conditions internal to
organizations, the people for whom they are providing a product or service, other organizations with whom they are com-
peting in the provision of this product or service, and current
and future economic, social, and political conditions that
have a bearing on the operations, plans, and goals of the organization. Applied specifically to business, this means that executives must set those goals for the company or corporation,
put together concepts, ideas, and specific plans for overcoming
opposition and attaining these goals in a unified strategy, determine short-range objectives as steps toward achieving goals,
develop an underlying company philosophy and set of policies,
design an organizational structure, obtain people to function
within this structure, implement procedures for the functioning of these people and standards for their performance, provide a plant and equipment, obtain money to finance operations
("working capital"), define and implement specific operational
management programs, furnish information on internal and
external developments to the people who are responsible for
programs, and take whatever action is necessary to put the
entire operation into motion.[6]

Strategic planning recognizes that all of these steps must
take into account that environments change as social, economic, and political forces shift. James Whittaker emphasizes this
and gets to the fundamental issues in strategic planning when
he says that this process centers on the way that resources are
allocated. Initially, he calls for an analysis of the environment
in which a business is operating. Specific opportunities and
threats are found through this analysis. The next action is to
evaluate the resources of the business firm to decide what is
available for design and implementation of a strategy that has a

chance for success with competitors in a particular market. The next step is to channel resources and skills so that they are related to a particular opportunity for which they are most appropriate. Deadlines for the attainment of specific company objectives are determined, and policies, plans, procedures, and specific responsibilities are created for the application of resources and attainment of goals.[7]

Both Steiner and Whittaker provide an extensive discussion of alternative planning models that attempt to consider all relevant internal and external factors influencing strategic planning. However, the essence of the strategic planning process has been captured in Steiner's *WOTS UP* acronym. The idea is that planners should discuss *w*eaknesses in their organization, *o*pportunities presented in the environment, *t*hreats that are apparent in terms of their organization, *s*trengths they believe their organization possesses, and the implications of these analyses for organizational planning.

This process involves a consideration of certain assumptions about the organization and the environment with respect to the future as well as the present. In the case of colleges and universities, this concern encompasses the goals of institutions and the needs of the clientele that the institutions expect to serve. The resources of the institution are important, but of equal significance are the needs of groups and individuals colleges and universities desire to serve. In business and industry a market analysis is undertaken to determine consumer needs. Assumptions are made concerning consumers, and plans are made accordingly. Matching of institutional resources and capabilities to deliver services is considered. If a college or university has the resources and philosophical commitment to deliver services related to consumer needs, alternative plans for the delivery of these services are weighed and an appropriate plan of action is determined. Programs in that area are promoted when it is decided that a market exists.

Comprehensive planning in higher education is a key aspect of decision making for future direction of institutional energy related to academic programs, physical plant and equipment, and financial operations. This process must be dynamic and continuous and characterized by constant assessment and reassessment of the future of the institution. It must consider all dimensions of academic, physical, and financial operations and the ways they relate to each other. Planning cannot be separated from financial considerations, specifically the process through which annual budgets evolve. Most significantly, planning is a management style in its own right. It can provide the dominant perspective on all decision making. This means that a major factor in the importance of planning at any given institution is the commitment of administration to this concept as a central concern of management.

While the values, commitments, and priorities of college and university chief executives are crucial in terms of the status assigned to planning, adequate data for making analyses, evaluations, and forecasts are vital to the success of planning whether this planning concerns day-to-day or strategic operations. The involvement of a broad range of persons in the planning process is also a critical issue. Planning must involve deans, directors, chairs, and others who are close to the implementation source of the plans. This level of participation must be combined with that of top-level executives, and the process of planning must consider external factors and conditions exerting a continuous influence on the directions of services, programs, policies, and practices in higher education.[8]

External factors and conditions of concern to planners include international and national political, economic, social, scientific, and technological developments. For example, decreases in the national birth rate, a reduction in the numbers of persons in the eighteen- to twenty-one-year age group, and a percentage decrease in the high school graduates entering higher education are significant factors for college and university planners. Unemployment and the resulting decrease in job opportunities for high school and college graduates influence planning in higher education. Other economic conditions are important because they affect the amount of money going to colleges and universities. In times of economic depression, sales and income tax dollars are down, and less money is available to appropriate to public colleges and universities. Charitable donations from individual, corporate, and foundation givers are also decreased. Political developments are closely related to eco-

nomic conditions, and a change in policy toward the provision
of student financial aid at state and federal government levels
has an important influence on the number of persons who are
able to attend colleges and universities. A shift in political
values of the country away from liberalism and commitment
to political and social justice and toward a more conservative,
individualistic, and self-centered position can mean that more
students are vocation- and career-oriented and less interested
in study in the humanities and social sciences. Academic programs, projects, and research are affected by federal government support of research and training in high technology and
scientific areas.[9] This support is influenced by international
political and economic conditions and concern for the national
defense. National defense relates to both financial support of
research and attendance pattern. These are only a few of the
developments planners must take into account, but their
mention should be sufficient to indicate the magnitude of the
problem of considering external factors in higher education.

Futures Research

Attempting to determine the direction these developments
will take in the future and other factors that might affect tomorrow's higher education are problems in the area of *futures
research*, a recently emerging field gaining increasing attention.
Through the futures approach certain assumptions and con-
tingencies are used to forecast what tomorrow may be like. The
environment of the future is simulated and various plans of
action relative to institutional goals, programs, and services are
"implemented" and "evaluated" on a "what if" basis. Efforts
are made to understand what the future might mean in terms
of alternative courses of action available and how these courses
of action might be affected by the elements of chance and choice.
Forecasting appears to be a fundamental expression in futures
research. A forecast is a statement made about the future with
a fair probability that it will be a reality if conditions in the
environment remain the same or do not change very rapidly.[10]
There are two types of forecasting with the first, *exploratory*
forecasting, being the more conservative of the two approaches,

since it considers the future as an extension of current trends
and their present implications. The exploratory forecaster
assumes the role of an objective observer. Present realities,
historical evidence, and future opportunities that might be
inferred from this information are analyzed. On the other hand,
normative forecasting, the second type, seems to require more
flexibility and creativity because the futures analyst in this
method must look into the future and project goals and objectives for the organization. When these goals and objectives
are determined, the analyst moves back to the present in an
attempt to decide on the best means for realizing these goals
and objectives that may have been projected into the future.
The values, beliefs, and hunches of the futures analyst are
more significant conditions in the case of normative forecasting, since a factual certainty that life will continue to be the
same is slight using this approach.[11] Both types of forecasting
need to be combined to attain the most effective results. Whether
these approaches are combined or applied separately, there are
certain appropriate techniques or methods for futures research.
Examples of these methods are: (1) Delphi method; (2) trend
extrapolation; (3) cross-impact analysis; (4) scenarios or future
histories; (5) morphological analysis; and (6) games, models,
and simulations.

Delphi method is a technique through which opinions from
experts are gained from a series of inquiries. An expert whose
opinion is solicited does not know opinions of specific other
experts whose opinions have also been sought. However, the
expert is told what opinions have been expressed without
identifying their individual sources, so that the expert might
have a basis for alteration or compromise. Compromises are
made possible on the basis of ideas and opinions not associated
with particular individuals. An individual's reputation, influence,
and charisma are not factors because interaction among experts is indirect and impersonal. Consensus is an objective, so
many feedback sessions or questionnaires are necessary as experts keep revising their responses on the basis of information
they are given on the responses of other experts. Measurable
results can be produced through this method. Other advantages
of this method over an open discussion are that a participant

ego won't be damaged through a public change of position and the going-along-with-the-group effect will not be as strong as in direct discussion.[12] The continual pushing for concensus, the privacy and protection from accountability for opinions, and the possibility that an expert may change an opinion just because it is contrary to the collective expert opinion, have been major criticisms of this method.[13]

Trend extrapolation, a less complex method than Delphi, is based on the assumption that social, political, and economic environments have some characteristics that are constant and mean that past, present, and future behavior remains the same. A trend is shown as a line on a graph, which extends over periods of time. Intervals of ten or twenty years, for example, are marked on this line, and the trend is examined at those intervals. An example of this method might be considering increases and decreases in unemployment, quantified and noted at intervals. The major defect in this technique is that it does not allow for change because it is based on the assumption that the past causes the future.

Cross-impact analysis is one attempt to meet the requirement that interrelationships and interdependence must be recognized. An event, whether it occurred in the past, is taking place now, or will happen in the future, never occurs in isolation from other events. Through this method events can be considered through a matrix on which they are evaluated as to their probability of taking place and the influence they will have on each other at certain points in time in the future. The events for cross-impact analysis are determined frequently through Delphi technique. For example, the Delphi experts might be asked to judge which events they believe will take place at some time in the future and to estimate the probability that these events will actually happen. Using this information, the futures analyst might consider the interaction of the Delphi experts' events and probabilities with a specific event the analyst is considering. The event, development, and implementation of a new curriculum in engineering technology might be inter-related with such events as enrollment increase, employment opportunities for graduates in the community, and renovation of physical facilities. For example, if the new curriculum is added, the probability of increases in opportunities for employment of graduates in the community could be considered.[14]

Scenarios or future histories are another futures research technique or method. Herman Kahn and Anthony J. Weiner have popularized the scenario method, which they define as:

> Hypothetical sequences of events constructed for the purpose of focusing attention on causal processes and decision points. They answer two kinds of questions: (1) Precisely how might some hypothetical situation come about, step by step? and (2) What alternatives exist for each actor, at each step, for preventing, diverting, or facilitating the process?[15]

The steps in a scenario can be taken from Delphi expert opinion as to important developments in the period for which the scenario is being written. A number of scenarios, each from the perspective of a different discipline, might be prepared for a particular period, and scenarios can be developed in conjunction with cross-impact analyses. The latter allows for an internal consistency check in which parts of the future history can be interrelated. Scenarios facilitate a consideration of any number of possibilities and creative alternatives.[16]

Morphological analysis concentrates on organization and interaction of the components in a system relating to a future state of affairs. The root word "morphology" comes from the biological sciences and refers to the study of structure and form. It resembles the systems approach but as it applies to futures research. Robert Kaufman refers to the systems approach in general as:

> A process by which needs are identified, problems selected, requirements for problem solution are identified, solutions are chosen from alternatives, methods and means are obtained and implemented, results are evaluated, and required revisions to all or part of the system are made so that needs are eliminated.[17]

The systems approach can be employed to analyze past events, solve current problems, and examine subject matter structurally

in a future situation. Morphological analysis has application
in the latter domain. It should be mentioned in this context
that morphological analysis is a method for establishing structure
and form for solving a problem as opposed to a technique designed to find a solution. This approach allows for a consideration
of as many possible factors, conditions, and alternative solutions
as the thinking and experience of futurists can conceive.

The strength of this approach also seems to be its weakness.
The perspectives or dimensions serving as components for examination are unlimited and depend upon the perception, imagination, and vision of the futures analyst. On the other hand,
these dimensions can be somewhat arbitrary since they cannot
be scrutinized and evaluated on a scientific basis. They can be
highly subjective.

Models, simulations, or *games,* other types of systems approaches to futures research might be established using a morphological analysis. Frequently these terms are presented in the
writing on higher education in various combinations through
such experssions as "simulation games" and "simulation model-
ing." Simulation games and models have important implications
for current as well as future problems. With respect to current
problems, an organization can use a management information
system (a bank of data on as many relevant facts, characteristics,
and other realities as possible which influence policies, programs,
and practices) to put together a vast amount of data related to
programs, services, resources, assumptions about environmental
conditions, a ranking of organizational goals, and many other
areas that influence the operations of the organization. Certain
data can be manipulated, and the effects of this manipulation
on various components of the system can be considered. In this
way, a contemplated change can be "run through" a model of
the actual system to determine possible consequences in microcosm prior to its actual implementation in the system or the
macrocosm itself.

In futures research language a *model* is a concept that represents an organization, plan, process, or subject area in a
more simplistic form than the phenomenon that it models.
Manipulating various parts of the model constitutes *simulation,*
and the exercise becomes a *game* when persons assume roles
in which they compete and cooperate with other role players,

who manipulate aspects of the model to attain certain ends.[18]

Advancements in computer technology have meant that sophisticated exercises can be undertaken and results attained in relatively short periods of time. This appears to be true for simulation models whether they are used for present or future situations. The computer serves as a storage place for vast amounts of information and it can retrieve information and perform mathematical and statistical procedures with astounding speed. Given certain priorities, values, conditions, and time sequences, it can present probable results or outcomes with the speed of light. These outcomes can be altered with equal rapidity as new information or changing conditions are given to the computer. The capability of the computer has made many methods and techniques in futures research feasible because of the speed with which sorting, correlating, and matching procedures can be accomplished. If done manually, such procedures are tedious, crude, and costly. With such techniques as relevance trees, decision trees, and contingency trees, computer technology makes possible myriads of comparisons of almost unlimited numbers of events and actions.

PPBS, ZBB, and MBO: Links Between Planning and Evaluation

Computer technology has also made possible extensive use of three management techniques that provide examples as to how planning and evaluation can merge into a continuous process. However, before discussing these examples, a definition of evaluation seems necessary to provide a basis for better understanding the relationship between planning and evaluation. The belief has been expressed that emphasis upon evaluation has come about in the public sector of higher education because taxpayers want to know how wisely and efficiently their money is being spent. A primary concern in this area relates to program and service evaluation, but the matter of evaluating the performance of persons who are responsible for these programs and services is also important. In practice it is difficult to separate evaluation of personnel involved in the success or failure of programs and services from the assessment of how well programs and services are accomplishing goals.

Scarvia Anderson and Samuel Ball state that the purposes of program evaluation go far beyond determining whether a program is "good" or not, and it is implied that evaluation also transcends the success or failure of personnel responsible for programs. These purposes usually can be categorized according to whether the end of the process is to: (1) determine effectiveness of an existing program; or (2) bring about the establishment of a new program. According to Anderson and Ball, the evaluation process is capable of: (1) providing information that can be used to decide whether a program should be installed; (2) furnishing evidence for a decision about maintaining, expanding, or certifying an existing program; (3) constituting a basis for program change; (4) rallying support for an existing program; (5) supplying information that can be used to oppose a program; and (6) adding to general knowledge of "basic psychological, social, and other processes."

The first capability suggested concerns determining need and demand, the conceptual and technical match of the program with need and demand, and whether human and material resources can meet need and demand. The second capability is to see if the program meets its goals in an effective manner and if the need and demand for which the program was established still exist. The competency of people responsible for the program and the adequacy and effectiveness of other dimensions of the system delivering the program can be assessed through the third capability of evaluation. Gathering information supporting the value, match, and efficiency of the program is a fourth evaluation capability. The converse of this, building up evidence against the program, is the fifth capability. The final capability, contributing to understanding of basic processes in the social sciences, is in addition to collecting information for a decision related to the specific program being evaluated.[19]

The approach of Anderson and Ball seems to be a realistic appraisal of the objectives and capacities of program evaluation, and it appears to have a number of characteristics in common with Richard Harpel's management model of evaluation. This model includes:

Identifying the problem (assessing needs)
Assessing environmental constraints

Stating goals
Defining objectives
Defining program structure
Budgeting
Assessing outcomes[20]

Planning, programming budget systems (PPBS), zero base
budgeting (ZBB), and management by objectives (MBO) incor-
porate the dimensions of Harpel's model in their procedures
in addition to reflecting Anderson and Ball's evaluation purposes. They also contain planning essentials discussed in the
initial section of this chapter. In other words, they illustrate
how planning and evaluation blend. The taxpayer demand for
wise and efficient use of public funds was cited as a reason
for evaluation. It has also been a contributing factor in attempts
to establish PPBS in American colleges and universities. This
concept gained major impetus in the early 1960s when Secretary of Defense Robert McNamara implemented PPBS in his
department of the United States government. Institutionalization
of the concept in entirety in business and educational enterprises has taken place rarely, but various phases and aspects of
it have been incorporated into the operations of virtually every
college and university in the United States.

John Millett believes that "planning-programming-budgeting
is an ordered procedure for setting forth objectives, activities,
and expenditure requirements."[21] The initial phase of PPBS,
planning, requires that the organization define its objectives
and develop a strategic plan for their accomplishment. These
goals must be realistic in terms of the human and material
resources of the organization. ZBB is highly similar to PPBS.
However, the basic premise for planning in the former is that
nothing can be taken for granted because of a previous year's
commitment or experience. The process starts from zero and
every proposed expense requires justification. There must be
a rationale for every program or activity that is covered by the
budget. Attention is given to alternative programs and activities
that might be funded to accomplish institutional objectives.
James Harvey specifies that the process concentrates upon
budget units that relate to these alternatives and form "deci-

sion packages." The most appropriate packages in terms of goals and priorities of the institution are selected for funding.[22]

Management by objectives (MBO) is used with PPBS at the time that objectives are determined and also when programs are evaluated as to their effectiveness in meeting these objectives. Through the MBO system, each manager or member of the institutional staff is supervised and evaluated on the basis of his or her accomplishment of specific measurable objectives predetermined through mutual agreement of the individual and his or her immediate superior. These personal objectives relate to the goals of programs, which have been derived from the overall purposes and objectives of the institution. Emphasis in this system is upon the achievement of clearly specified goals to be accomplished usually in a yearly time period, and it concentrates upon the results of activities rather than the activities themselves.[23]

During the planning phase of PPBS, when a strategic plan is developed, a planning model representing what the institution is supposed to be like over a longer period (probably five or ten years) is structured. This model serves as a gauge for determining whether programs and activities are meeting their objectives. The defining and clarifying of institutional goals are crucial since clarifications and definitions establish direction for the determination of specific programs and services and form the basis for evaluation. Robert Pavese believes that information necessary to determine institutional objectives should include: (1) the current curriculum and that planned for the next decade; (2) degrees being conferred and any new degrees contemplated for the future; (3) characteristics of current and future students; (4) admissions requirements, present and future; (5) time allowed for students to complete degree requirements; (6) the relationship of the college or university to its external community; (7) expectations for faculty in terms of instruction, research, public service, and other activities; (8) advantages gained by students who complete degree requirements; (9) roles of internal and external governing groups; (10) financial support received by the institution from state, federal, and private sources; (11) the programs and plans of other colleges and universities, especially those in the immediate community; and (12) arrangements of interinstitutional co-operation with colleges and universities in the community.[24]

Sources of these data may be legislative enactments, institutional charters, records of minutes of boards of regents and boards of trustees, faculty council and committee reports, institutional academic and financial master plans, reports and recommendations from evaluating committees and consultants, and research and study findings from private, state, and federal agencies and groups. For PPBS purposes, one document should provide a basis for an integration of all of this information, and this document should serve as a guide for the approval and establishment of policies and procedures leading to the attainment of institutional objectives.[25]

The accomplishment of institutional objectives is undertaken through specific programs and services. These programs and services require certain institutional resources or inputs. These inputs can be further defined as financial and nonfinancial resources that are necessary to support the instructional, research, and public service missions of the institution and the programs through which these missions are accomplished. These resources are the people who work for the college or university. Their responsibilities, work loads, and salaries or wages should be considered. These human resources include all ranks of professors, instructors, lecturers, teaching fellows and graduate assistants, managers and administrators, clerical personnel, librarians, and custodial, maintenance, grounds, and security employees. Resources also encompass students and a consideration of their majors and full- or part-time status. This consideration extends to class size ratios and the number of students in each instructional program. Another input consideration relates to the number of courses in which students can enroll. Descriptions of courses are also a part of this input. Other resources are equipment, supplies, furnishings, materials, physical facilities such as classrooms, laboratories, faculty offices, study areas, and libraries which can be inventoried with respect to their square footage, total number, and utilization.[26]

The production of these inputs might be evaluated according to outputs, which are defined as (1) number and variety of academic degrees awarded by the institution; (2) number of

credit courses, including number of students enrolled and
credit-hour value of each; (3) volumes in the library; (4) research
grants received by the faculty and scholarly publications produced; (5) community service activities, including cultural,
artistic, and dramatic events and exhibits, lectures, and urban
and community projects; (6) performance of students on
standardized examinations given to freshmen, seniors, and
applicants for admission to graduate programs; (7) graduate
school admissions of seniors from the institution; (8) alumni
performance, including positions held, salaries, promotions,
participation in community activities, and advanced academic
work (alumni evaluations of the institution may be included);
(9) assessments of institutional programs by accrediting agencies;
and (10) self-study evaluations by committees of institutional
faculty, administration, and staff.[27]

Alternative programs and services and different arrangements
of financial and nonfinancial resources are considered through
the PPBS approach. A formal system of procedures, which
furnishes input data and other symbolic information is essential
for decision making in all phases of PPBS. In planning and
decision making this system is referred to as a management
information system (MIS). Harry J. Hartley states that MIS:

> Integrates the dynamic functions of an organiza-
> tion, such as instruction, personnel and finance,
> and provides computer-aided systems of informa-
> tion control for administrators; it may be a report-
> ing system or a decision making system, depending
> on level of application.[28]

MIS is especially useful at that stage when alternatives, or in
Harvey's terms *decision packages*, are being selected. Before a
particular decision package is chosen, a number of packages
are developed. The decision package is the final product of a
process that begins with the formulation of a broad mission
statement. From that statement a goal is derived, and an objective is specified from the goal. A program is developed to
accomplish the objective, and the program is divided into
decision units. Decision packages can then be designed around

decision units. A *mission statement* is an encompassing declaration of what an organization is attempting to accomplish.
While this specification of purpose is broad, it still establishes
boundaries for organizational activities. A *goal* derived from
a mission statement refers to a single desired purpose or condition. It is of a general nature and appropriate for the organization for an indefinite period of time. Even though a goal
itself is not quantifiable, specific objectives can be formulated
from that goal. An *objective* is a precise statement about a
specific condition or achievement that is desired. A period of
time is specified for its accomplishment. An objective must
have a measurable quality so that a "yes or no" decision can
be made as to whether it has been attained during the time
specified. A *program* covers all activities planned and carried
out to accomplish an objective or combination of objectives.
A program can be considered as a *decision unit*, which is a
component of a budget around which alternative activities can
be clustered. When costs of accomplishing each of these
activities are assigned, these activities become *decision packages*.
The successful application of ZBB requires that each decision
package be carefully defined and detailed, so that the best
of at least three options for each decision unit can be selected.[29]
Examples of decision units for which decision packages might
be prepared are (1) in the general area of instruction—divisions
or departments, courses, academic administration, faculty
development, overseas programs, computer-assisted instruction,
instructional support, and remedial or developmental education;
(2) in the area of administration: office of the president, alumni
relations, computer services, legal service, university relations;
(3) learning resources center area: cataloging, new book purchases,
photocopy and microfilm, and bookbinding; (4) in the area of
student services: admissions, registration, student records, counseling, student activities, and career development and placement;
and (5) in the business affairs area: accounting, purchasing,
buildings and grounds, campus police, payroll, trust funds, and
controller's office.[30]

   Programs for Pavese are similar to Harvey's decision units.
To illustrate what is meant by a program, Pavese uses the example of an undergraduate liberal arts college specifying eight

general program areas, which might contain a number of sub-
programs or program elements. The first three program areas
are for direct instruction in the humanities, life and physical
sciences, and social sciences. A fourth program area covers
services to the divisions of humanities, life and physical
sciences, and social sciences, and it includes the operations of
admissions, the registrar, the bursar, counseling, library, and
data processing. Pavese's fifth program area is for student,
faculty, and staff service (food service, housing, financial aid,
recreation, health service, parking, and entertainment); his
sixth program area relates to public services, and research and
development are the subjects of the seventh area. The last
program area is residual and is for general support. The general
support program area includes such units as the board of
trustees, the president's office, financial administration, fund
raising, alumni relations, personnel administration, public
relations, institutional memberships, professional fees, plant
operation and maintenance for support units, fringe benefits
for support units, and debt service not directly charged to other
programs.[31]

Institutional inputs, such as personnel employed, class size
ratios, supplies, equipment and furnishings, and other financial
and nonfinancial resources already described, are related to these
program areas in the planning phase of PPBS. Sources of income,
such as that from tuition and fees, state and federal funds, service charges, and private gifts and grants should "be identified
and applied to the program earning the income" in the planning
phase.[32]

When decisions have been made as to the course of action
to be taken or, in Harvey's terms, the best "decision package"
is selected, the program is executed. It is evaluated as it is in
operation on the basis of its "outputs," which are checked
against the objectives for which the program was planned.
Extensive data to do this monitoring makes MIS as important
in the evaluation stage as it is for planning. Unfortunately,
many colleges and universities appear to be unwilling to spend
the money for technical staff necessary to evaluate alternative
programs during the planning stage and also during the evaluation phase of PPBS. Charles Schultze, former Director of the

Federal Bureau of the Budget, has indicated problems in the
implementation and operation of PPBS. He points to the initial
problem of evaluating qualitative results of education in dollars
and cents terms and other quantifiable measures. Higher education has multiple costs, and it is difficult to divide these costs
into distinct categories. Schultze also emphasizes that frequently
political bargaining processes and PPBS do not accommodate
each other. Endemic to establishing priorities for objectives
and programs are political opportunity costs, and the implications and consequences of policy decisions are often difficult
to predict.[33]

Methods of Evaluation

In spite of weaknesses pointed out by Charles Schultze,
evaluation must be attempted. It remains a critical dimension of
any plan or program. Methods selected for evaluation relate to
purposes. Is the purpose of evaluation to determine effectiveness and results of a new program which is in the process of
development, or is the purpose to see if an already fully developed program is accomplishing its objective? This particular
distinction has been made by Michael Scriven who calls the
first type of evaluation *formative*, and the second, *summative*.[34]
Whether rationale for evaluation is guided by formative or
summative purposes, political considerations are foremost, and
the success of any evaluative technique depends upon the
awareness of the evaluator to politics. One of the reasons for
increased emphasis on evaluation has been taxpayer and legislator concern over the constantly rising costs of education.
Greater responsibility and accountability have been placed upon
educational leaders (college and university presidents, vice
presidents, deans, and directors), and they have been required
to demonstrate the quantitative value of higher education.[35]
This concern means that results are significant. Results ema-
nating from a system or process need to be judged in terms of
meeting program or organizational ends and political considerations. A number of methods have been devised to accomplish
both academic and political objectives. Anderson and Ball present the following general investigative methods as appropriate

approaches to program evaluation. These methods are worthy of discussion from both scientific and political perspectives. They include:

1. Experimental studies
2. Quasi-experimental studies
3. Correlational status studies
4. Surveys
5. Personnel or client assessment
6. Systematic expert judgment
7. Clinical or case studies
8. Informal observation or testimony[36]

If rationality and objectivity are the guides, a clear sense of direction emerges with respect to the methods employed in evaluative research. This "clear sense of direction," however, is contingent upon the belief that absolute controls can be established and maintained to avoid contamination from conditions, happenings, and trends in the real world. The assumption is that the test-tube model can be applied. This implies that at least two laboratory groups can be defined with the minimum condition that a *control* group and an *experimental* group are possible. What goes into each "test tube" is absolutely the same, and all other influencing developments can be controlled. Contents of both tubes are measured and recorded. They must be the same at the beginning of the experiment or evaluation. Then the action, program, or treatment that is the subject of measurement is introduced, or placed, in the experimental tube and *not* in the control tube. After the two tubes have been "shaken up," the resulting comparison is measured. If there are differences, it is reasonable to conclude that the action, program, or treatment made the difference.

A method that approaches this model, but requires qualification in interpreting some results because of some characteristic or development that could not be controlled or some type of generalized assumption inherent in its processes, seems to be given quasi-experimental status.

Correlational methods enter the realm of cause-and-effect relationships. Probably any kind of reliable conclusion here is in the strictly controlled laboratory experiment. When human beings and human groups are subjects, any conclusions in this area are wrought with problems. This is always dangerous ground in social science. It is just plain impossible to control!

Surveys that generate data on individual opinions related to satisfaction or dissatisfaction with a particular program produce results that appear to relate directly to the intent of the survey and the sheer numbers of individuals who respond. If the goal of a program is to meet what the *subjects* of the program *think* their needs are, then the evaluation objective is to ask as many of those subjects as possible what they believe the program did for them.

Client or participant judgment provides one dimension for evaluation. Another perspective on the effectiveness of a program comes from the judgment of experts. People who have status and established reputations in program areas can be called in to make judgments and render opinions. The validity of subjective or objective evidence depends upon the orientations of the people who are supposed to make judgments. Their orientations concerning evaluation and their personal value systems are determining factors.

The use of case studies to provide evidence of program effectiveness has limitations. Anderson and Ball state:

> The concern here, as with formal observation or testimony, is that if the aggregation is not systematic, any generalized decisions may be over-reactions. Five cases of serious contagious disease over a short period in a given locale may be shocking but, without more information than the fact of the five cases, the government might not be justified in setting up a massive immunization program.[37]

However, if the administrator responsible for innoculations is affected directly by one of these five cases, objectivity and the general welfare become relatively insignificant. Statistical evidence may be outweighed by personal emotion with the result that an extensive program is implemented. In a similar area of reasoning, informal observation and testimony take on

major significance when the informal observers and "testifiers"
are people in positions of power. In reality, with respect to
decisions and programs, their opinions override any kind of
empirical evidence available.

The truth is that if the results of these methods of evaluation
are to be useful in program modification or any kind of effort
to meet needs and goals better, communication to the people
who can bring about changes is essential. A major problem in
the public sector of higher education is that people too often
do not understand evaluation reports. It is a crucial matter
because the public pays tax dollars to support higher education.
Evaluators develop a particular jargon, which may make them
feel good about themselves as professionals and applied scientists,
and it may create mysticism around their cult. It might even be
argued, with respect to communication, that this jargon is
characterized by an inconsistency in the use of certain terms,
which causes confusion and misunderstanding even in the
inner circles of these planners and evaluators. If evaluation
studies are to make a difference, evaluators must write their
reports for their audiences, and this involves knowing the power
structure and idiosyncrasies and interests of decision makers.

Robert D. Brown offers "ten commandments" that are not
only applicable to the report of an evaluation study, but also
to the entire process of evaluation. He directs the evaluator to
(1) know who decision makers are; (2) identify key issues;
(3) identify sources of resistance and conflict; (4) make the
content of the evaluation relevant; (5) get the staff involved
in planning and evaluation (involvement of people who will
be affected by policies and decisions in the planning process
before decisions are actually made means that they can take
on ownership in the process); (6) focus the evaluation on
the problem rather than on the personnel; (7) understand the
administrator's role; (8) clarify expectations; (9) establish
credibility; and (10) be humble.[38]

Summary

The scientific method in education has implications for
management decisions and policies as it does for exercises in

the classroom. It means that planners must clarify educational
objectives, determine the needs of persons and groups that
education is to serve, devise programs and services for meeting
the needs of people when the meeting of these needs is consistent with institutional missions and resources, evaluate programs and services against this need base, and continually
modify and improve programs and services to meet constituent
needs. People in positions of power should, therefore, establish
procedures so that all persons affected by decisions and policies
have the chance to express their ideas and opinions before
decisions are actually made and policies are formalized. This
is a vital part of any planning process.

Planners have become important influences on higher education in the decade of the 1980s. In fact, these people who
emphasize quantification and measurement from a business-
engineering-technology perspective exert a significant influence
on American society as a whole. That perspective and attempts
to apply the scientific method with equal precision to all problems
exemplify the problem of overquantification and the dangers
inherent in such an approach, if it is not constantly questioned
and checked by other special interest groups. President John H.
Marburger, III, of the State University of New York at Stony
Brook, has raised the point that some ignorance is inevitable
in college and university operations as well as in broader realms
of human affairs. Not all life is knowable, quantifiable, measurable, and predictable. To apply a language from the physical
sciences and mathematics to a number of problem areas in
higher education implies a rationality and solvability that do
not exist. He states:

> The predictive success of science has been so great
> that efforts have been made in every other practical
> field to introduce scientific methods. The results
> have been useful, but outside physical science
> reliable predictions can be achieved only in the
> simplest situations. Even where we do not have a
> clear understanding of the relation between means
> and ends, however, we use language patterned after
> the more successful sciences to describe events.

> This encourages the illusion among the inexpert
> that we know more than we do. Medicine has em-
> ployed this practice with success for millennia.[39]

Marburger argues that understanding some aspects of life and
survival in uncertain times and unpredictable situations are the
results of education in the humanities rather than in the sciences.
The flexible, imaginative human mind can be as essential for the
survival of society as precise efforts to quantify and predict.

The position of planners and evaluators must be kept within
its proper perspective. This special interest group has no better
insight on the interests of the public than any other faction in
society because of the nature of the public. The concept of *a*
public or commonwealth is an ideal rather than a reality. In
actuality there is *no* commonwealth or public, only a spectrum
of beliefs concerning what is best for people in general as held
by individuals and groups on the basis of their special interests,
roles in society, needs, and values, all the result of social experience. The first chapter of this book presented the argument
that a principal dimension of knowledge is subjective and
related to individual beliefs and assumptions because of differences in perception and social experience. The application of
fundamental sociology extends this perspective of the individual
to groups.

While general social, economic, and political systems as determinants of behavior have gained increasing importance, social
groups and the roles and statuses individuals hold in those groups
are major factors in how individuals respond to broader system
conditions and developments. People discuss major issues and
developments with their friends and others who exert an influence
on their lives. People are what they are because of the social
groups with whom they have contact. Ideas, attitudes, values,
needs, interests, and opinions are formed as a result of these
contacts. These contacts are limited in general by socioeconomic
and cultural circumstances. In the early decades of the 1900s,
University of Chicago sociologists established a high water mark
in the interpretation of this position. Improvements have been
largely semantic with some refinements taking place, but the
basic theory holds.

When people view any situation and make interpretations, their reactions are on the basis of their values, beliefs, goals, and experiences. People with similar backgrounds, interests, and objectives tend to have similar views and to support each other in efforts to attain goals. This was recognized in the Constitution of the United States through a system of checks and balances. It should be better recognized in American higher education. All of the many groups who have an interest in higher education view that enterprise from a distinct perspective, from a special interest vantage point, and to expect any person or group to have *the general welfare* perspective is a sociological impossibility.

This is not to say that consensus cannot be realized concerning general directions or that broad, intergroup beliefs that something is wrong are impossible. Even though individual special interest groups have their own interpretations pertaining to general directions and action which is necessary, there can be a widespread recognition that change is needed. Proposition 13 in California may be a good example. Many special interest groups in that state arrived at the conclusion that taxpayers were being overburdened in the support of public services. The history of higher education furnishes other examples which show that general external needs and forces have influenced programs and services offered by colleges and universities and the people to whom these programs and services have been offered.

While general trends appear and broad notions arise that change is needed, prescriptions for action are determined by special interests, usually those groups whose approaches offer a solution for the problems sensed by the general society. However, the pendulum tends to swing back and forth with one bandwagon effect being countered by another in the opposite direction.

In the United States, the swinging of the pendulum seems to have been perpetuated by the establishment of a system of checks and balances. In politics and just about every other area featured by competition among special interest groups, checks and balances are expected to provide a balance and to keep the pendulum from swinging too radically. However, as has been pointed out in Chapter 1, in the American system advantages go to those groups with the finances and resources required to take advantage of opportunities and rights. The government does not intervene on behalf of groups that are unable to assert their rights and capitalize on opportunities available to them. Rights are not guaranteed, only opportunities to secure them.

It is difficult in government to ensure that *all* special interest groups are allowed to compete on equal footing. Such assurance would require a drastic change in the system that now prevails. Financial means are requisite for any substantial influence. At all levels, individuals who are candidates for public office need money and support in general from moneyed interests to gain office. Political campaigns are costly but necessary to win elections. In higher education, the situation is somewhat different. Most positions on boards of trustees or regents in public institutions are of an appointed nature. To gain broader special interest group representation, it could be prescribed through legislation that as many special interest groups as possible be represented on boards. The appointments made by governors could be limited to representatives from these groups. Designation of specific groups would be difficult, since a myriad of interest groups is possible depending upon issues, but efforts to make these determinations would at least be a start and an attempt to accomplish an ideal of higher education in the public sector. The inordinate influences of corporate power, militarization, racism, sexism, and overquantification might even be affected.

Concerning the special interest groups which are internal to colleges and universities, measures need to be taken to ensure that faculty, students, staff, and the various special interests within these groups are involved in the formulation of programs, policies, practices, and procedures at all levels. This is necessary to establish checks and balances on the diversity of perspectives, which are significant inside colleges and universities. It is also necessary to furnish a militating force for administrative influence.

The method for the accomplishing this objective may vary from institution to institution, depending upon current and

historical circumstances. In some cases collective bargaining
may be the most appropriate means while in others consideration of faculty senates, student councils, nonacademic employee councils, and all-university councils is more important. Whatever means are used to establish involvement and participation
from groups internal to colleges and universities, roles must be
spelled out and special interests recognized for both their limitations and strengths.

Only through an honest recognition of the limitations of
human beings and human groups, both internal and external
to colleges and universities, can American higher education
ever hope to accomplish its broad objectives.

Notes

1. Jacob Bronowski, *Science and Human Values* (New York: Harper
Torchbooks, 1956), pp. 60-61.

2. René Descartes, "Discourse on Method," translated by John Veitch,
in *The Rationalists* (Garden City, New York: Doubleday, 1960), pp.
58-59.

3. Mortimer Chambers, Raymond Grew, David Herlihy, Theodore K.
Rabb, and Isser Woloch, *The Western Experience*, vol. 3, *The Modern
Era* (New York: Alfred A. Knopf, 1971), pp. 1005-1006.

4. J. Donald Butler, *Four Philosophies of Education and Their Practice in Education and Religion* (New York: Harper and Brothers, 1957),
p. 333.

5. George A. Steiner, *Strategic Planning: What Every Manager Must
Know* (New York: Free Press, 1979), pp. 4-5.

6. Marvin Bower, *The Will to Manage, Corporate Success Through
Programmed Management* (New York: McGraw-Hill, 1966), pp. 17-18.

7. James B. Whittaker, *Strategic Planning in a Rapidly Changing Environment* (Lexington, Massachusetts: Lexington Books, 1978), pp. 3-4.

8. William F. Lasher, "The Comprehensive Institutional Planning Process and the Role of Information In It," *Planning for Higher Education* 6,
no. 4 (February 1978).

9. Frederick R. Brodzinski, "The Futurist Perspective and the Managerial Process," in *Utilizing Futures Research*, ed. Frederick R. Brodzinski
(San Francisco: Jossey-Bass, 1979), p. 26.

10. Robert D. Ayers, *Technological Forecasting and Long Range Planning* (New York: McGraw-Hill, 1969), p. xii.

11. Harvey Welch, Jr., and Sally E. Watson, "Techniques of Futures

Research," in *Utilizing Futures Research*, ed. Frederick R. Brodzinski
(San Francisco: Jossey-Bass, 1979), p. 3.

12. Stuart A. Sandow, "The Pedagogy of Planning: Defining Sufficient
Futures," *Futures* 3 (December 1971): 325.

13. Welch and Watson, "Techniques of Futures Research," p. 7.

14. Sandow, "The Pedagogy of Planning: Defining Sufficient Futures,"
p. 332.

15. Herman Kahn and Anthony J. Weiner, *The Year 2000: A Frame-
work for Speculation on the Next Thirty-Three Years* (New York: Macmillan, 1967), p. 6.

16. Welch and Watson, "Techniques of Futures Research," p. 10.

17. Robert A. Kaufman, *Educational System Planning* (Englewood
Cliffs, New Jersey: Prentice-Hall, 1972), p. 2.

18. Welch and Watson, "Techniques of Futures Research," p. 13.

19. Scarvia B. Anderson and Samuel Ball, *The Profession and Practice
of Program Evaluation* (San Francisco: Jossey-Bass, 1978), pp. 3-4.

20. Richard I. Harpel, "Evaluating From a Management Perspective,"
in *Evaluating Program Effectiveness*, ed. Gary R. Hanson (San Francisco:
Jossey-Bass, 1978), pp. 20-32.

21. John D. Millett, *Planning, Programming and Budgeting for Ohio's
Public Institutions of Higher Education* (Columbus, Ohio: Ohio Board
of Regents, 1970), pp. 1-2.

22. L. James Harvey, *Zero Base Budgeting in Colleges and Universities*
(Littleton, Colorado: Ireland Educational Corporation, 1977), p. 7

23. Ibid., p. 6.

24. Robert Pavese, "Program Budgeting in Higher Education," in *Educational Planning-Programming-Budgeting: A Systems Approach* by Harry
J. Hartley (Englewood Cliffs, New Jersey: Prentice-Hall, 1968), p. 213.

25. Ibid., pp. 213-214.

26. Ibid., pp. 221-222.

27. Ibid., pp. 222-223.

28. Harry J. Hartley, *Educational Planning-Programming-Budgeting:
A Systems Approach* (Englewood Cliffs, New Jersey: Prentice-Hall, 1968),
p. 255.

29. Harvey, *Zero Base Budgeting in Colleges and Universities*, pp. 5-7.

30. Ibid., p. 42.

31. Pavese, "Program Budgeting in Higher Education," pp. 218-221.

32. Ibid., p. 223.

33. Charles Schultze, "PPBS in Higher Education," speech delivered
at Santa Cruz Seminar, University of California at Santa Cruz, August 1969.

34. Bruce W. Tuckman, *Conducting Educational Research* (New York:
Harcourt Brace Jovanovich, 1972), p. 325.

35. David Jesser, "Educational Research and the Educational Research-er," in *Methods and Techniques of Educational Research*, ed. Ralph H. Jones (Danville, Illinois: Interstate Printers and Publishers, 1973), p. 484.

36. Anderson and Ball, *The Profession and Practice of Program Evaluation*, pp. 43-66.

37. Ibid., p. 62.

38. Robert D. Brown, "How Evaluation Can Make a Difference," in *Evaluating Program Effectiveness*, ed. Gary R. Hanson (San Francisco: Jossey-Bass, 1979), p. 68.

39. John H. Marburger III, "Point of View: How to Cope With In-evitable Ignorance: The Humanities Can Give Some Answers," *Chronicle of Higher Education*, September 9, 1981, p. 72.

BIBLIOGRAPHIC ESSAY

Complete footnotes for references are listed after every chapter. However, certain resources should be cited because of their special significance for the reader.

In the case of special influences on higher education, Jerome H. Skolnik and Elliott Curries's *Crisis in American Institutions*, while published in 1970, still provides excellent background on the affects of racism, corporate power, and militarization. Lewis M. Killian's *The Impossible Revolution, Elusive Equality* by Lorenzo Morris, and Marcia G. Synnott's *The Half-Opened Door* are helpful with respect to understanding racism. Floyd Hunter's controversial *Community Power Structure* and *Top Leadership, U.S.A.* are important readings on corporate power and wealth when balanced with Robert A. Dahl's *Who Governs?* Sumner Rosen's *Economic Power Failure* is also valuable in this area. Betty Friedan's *The Feminine Mystique* remains as one of the best references for understanding the broad implications of sexism in the United States. Joan Abramson's *The Invisible Woman* and Betty Richardson's *Sexism in Higher Education* show what this might mean for higher education.

John Locke's "An "Essay Concerning Human Understanding" and David Hume's "An Enquiry Concerning Human Understanding," both in *Great Books of the Western World*, volume 35, provide a basis for understanding the tentative nature of knowledge and the dangers of overquantification. Steven C. Jessie's unpublished dissertation, "The Nature of Knowledge and Its Implications for Mental Health," also furnishes considerable insight.

The external governance of higher education today is covered extensively in *Handbook of College and University Trusteeship* edited by Richard T. Ingram. Contributions by George W. Angell and Edward P. Kelley, Jr., John J. Corson, Ingram, John W. Nason, and John D. Millett are especially appropriate for this chapter.

E. G. Bogue and Robert L. Saunders's *The Educational Manager*, unfortunately out of print, is an excellent consideration of educational administration in general. Michael D. Cohen and James G. March's *Leadership and Ambiguity* lends insight into special problems of the college presidency, and John J. Corson's *The Governance of Colleges and Universities: Modernizing Structure and Processes* examines a broad area of practices and problems in internal governance. J. Victor Baldridge's *Power and Conflict in the University* is one of the most realistic approaches to characteristics and conditions of the academic environment and their implications for governance. *Chairing the Academic Department* by Allan Tucker is an up-to-date discussion of leadership at the departmental level.

The changing situation in the funding of higher education is such that the best references appear to be the *Chronicle of Higher Education, Journal of Higher Education*, and other periodicals that keep pace with current developments. However, Merritt M. Chambers' *Higher Education: Who Pays? Who Gains?*, though outdated in some respects, provides a good general history of funding.

College and Univeristy Business Administration, the "bible" of the National Association of College and University Business Officers, is the key reference for business and financial operations.

The *Handbook of Institutional Advancement* edited by A. Westley Rowland covers a wide range of topics in the area of development. Leonard W. Bucklin's chapter is a good discussion of the important area of deferred giving. Chapters by Jack R. Bohlen and Conrad Teitell in Asa S. Knowles's *Handbook of College and University Administration*, volume 1, are helpful in understanding the development area and deferred giving, respectively.

For the subject of accreditation, *Private Accrediting and Public Eligibility* by Harold Orlans and others is a comprehensive reference. Franklin Patterson's *Colleges in Consort* is important in understanding the development and status of interinstitutional cooperation.

No one reference was found that provides a comprehensive treatment of public service in universities, community service in two-year institutions, and community education, but J. Martin Klotsche's *The Urban University* is a good discussion of issues and potentials related to public service in the public four-year urban institution. *Reaching Out Through Community Service* edited by Hope M. Holcomb presents an adequate discussion of community services in two-year colleges, especially in the chapters by William A. Keim and John M. Nickens. James F. Gollattscheck, Ervin L. Harlacher, Eleanor Roberts, and Benjamin R. Wygal's *College Leadership for Community Renewal* is another important reference for that area. Community education is presented in current and historical context by Maurice F. Seay et al. in *Community Education: A Developing Concept*.

For the chapter on planning and evaluation, the most important references are George A. Steiner's *Strategic Planning: What Every Manager Should Know*, James B. Whittaker's *Strategic Planning in a Rapidly Changing Environment*, Scarvia B. Anderson and Samuel Ball's *The Profession and Practice of Program Evaluation*, and Robert Pavese's chapter on "Program Budgeting in Higher Education" in Harry J. Hartley's *Educational Planning-Programming-Budgeting: A Systems Approach*. L. James Harvey's *Zero Base Budgeting in Colleges and Universities* presents a concise discussion of that concept and relates it to management by objectives and planning, programming budget systems. Stuart A. Sandow's article, "The Pedagogy of Planning: Defining Sufficient Futures" in *Futures* is useful in gaining a basic understanding of futures research.

In conclusion, John S. Brubacher and Willis Rudy's *Higher Education in Transition: A History of American Colleges and Universities, 1636-1976* is an excellent general historical reference which establishes a wide background perspective for higher education in the United States today, and the *Chronicle of Higher Education* continues to be highly appropriate for keeping abreast of current developments.

An overall perspective for the interpretation of a substantial segment of the information presented by Brubacher and Rudy, the *Chronicle of Higher Education*, and the chapters in this book is presented in Earl Latham's statement on "The Group Basis of Politics" in *American Political Interest Groups: Readings in Theory and Research* edited by Betty H. Zisk. While he explains and establishes the significance of special interest groups in politics, the implications of what he says for the politics of higher education are readily apparent, especially to those who have any extensive experience in college and university administration and teaching. Special interests must be considered in just about all that takes place in American higher education.

INDEX

Abelard, Peter, 184
Academic department(s): as central unit, 62-64; role of chair, 63-64; as self-serving, 31
Academic freedom: and special interests, 29; and faculty, 57-59
Academic standards, 28
Academic support, 98
Accounting, 94-104; classifications in, 98; and chief business officer, 96; for investments, 96
Accreditation: current status of, 144-146; definition of, 141; and federal funding, 144; and licensing, 143, 157; major problems in, 146-151; origins of, 142-144; principles for, 141, 143-144; for proprietary schools, 146; recommendations for, 141, 146-150; regional agencies for, 145; significance of, 32, 139-141, 157; for special programs, 146
Accrediting Commission for Junior Colleges of the Western States, 170
Accrediting Council on Education in Journalism and Mass Communications, 150
Accrual accounting: definition of, 102; as significant for colleges and universities, 96
Adams, John, 13
Administration. See Management
Administrative procedures acts (APA), 37-38

Admission standards, 28, 59
Adult(s): characteristics of, 161-163; and community education, 172; education of and federal funding, 73; education of, requiring new approaches, 164
Adult Education Association of the U.S.A., 173
Advisory coordinating boards, 33
Affirmative action, 120. See also Racism; Sexism
Agency Funds, 97, 100
Agriculture: and federal funding, 72; and Hatch Act of 1887, 70; and Morrill Act of 1862, 70
Akron, University of, 153
Alabama: construction of private college facilities, 78; governance of higher education, 33
Alabama, University of, 125
Alaska: funding of higher education, 79; governance of higher education, 34
Alumni: financial contributions, 82; importance, 134; influence, 28-29; involvement in internal governance, 67; loyalty, 117
Alumni relations: and beliefs and emotions, 114-115; as institutional advancement, 119
American Association for Leisure and Recreation, 173
American Association for the Ad-

About the Author

E. C. WALLENFELDT is Associate Professor of Educational Administration at Kent State University where he received the Distinguished Teaching Award in 1980. He has served in various administrative positions at the University of Iowa, Milton College, the University of Wisconsin-Oshkosh, and Cleveland State University. His articles have appeared in the *NASPA Journal* and the *Journal of the National Association of Women Deans and Counselors.*